1st EDITION

Perspectives on Modern World History

The *Challenger* Disaster

1st EDITION

Perspectives on Modern World History

The *Challenger* Disaster

Sylvia Engdahl

Editor

GREENHAVEN PRESS
A part of Gale, Cengage Learning

Detroit • New York • San Francisco • New Haven, Conn • Waterville, Maine • London

Elizabeth Des Chenes, *Director, Content Strategy*
Cynthia Sanner, *Publisher*
Douglas Dentino, *Manager, New Product*

© 2014 Greenhaven Press, a part of Gale, Cengage Learning.

Gale and Greenhaven Press are registered trademarks used herein under license.

For more information, contact:
Greenhaven Press
27500 Drake Rd.
Farmington Hills, MI 48331-3535
Or you can visit our Internet site at gale.cengage.com.

ALL RIGHTS RESERVED.
No part of this work covered by the copyright herein may be reproduced, transmitted, stored, or used in any form or by any means graphic, electronic, or mechanical, including but not limited to photocopying, recording, scanning, digitizing, taping, Web distribution, information networks, or information storage and retrieval systems, except as permitted under Section 107 or 108 of the 1976 United States Copyright Act, without the prior written permission of the publisher.

For product information and technology assistance, contact us at
Gale Customer Support, 1-800-877-4253.

For permission to use material from this text or product, submit all requests online at
www.cengage.com/permissions.

Further permissions questions can be e-mailed to permissionrequest@cengage.com.

Articles in Greenhaven Press anthologies are often edited for length to meet page requirements. In addition, original titles of these works are changed to clearly present the main thesis and to explicitly indicate the author's opinion. Every effort is made to ensure that Greenhaven Press accurately reflects the original intent of the authors. Every effort has been made to trace the owners of copyrighted material.

Cover image © Roger Ressmeyer/Corbis and © Everett Collection Historical/Alamy.

LIBRARY OF CONGRESS CATALOGING-IN-PUBLICATION DATA

The Challenger disaster / Sylvia Engdahl, book editor.
    pages cm. -- (Perspectives on modern world history)
    Includes bibliographical references and index.
    ISBN 978-0-7377-6365-2 (hardcover)
    1. Space vehicle accidents--United States. 2. Challenger (Spacecraft)--Accidents. I. Engdahl, Sylvia, editor of compilation.
    TL867.C44 2013
    363.12'4--dc23   2013005279

Printed in the United States of America
1 2 3 4 5 6 7 17 16 15 14 13

A12006 017216

CONTENTS

Hampshire. While the students initially celebrated when *Challenger* launched because their popular and inspiring teacher, Christa McAuliffe, was aboard, the cheers turned to silence at the announcement of the tragedy.

CHAPTER 2   Controversies Concerning the *Challenger* Disaster made people realize how dangerous it is. But human exploration of the universe is important, the editorial maintains, and the heroes who died would want it to continue.

he wondered if he could have done more to stop the launch, and how he was viewed as a whistleblower and had trouble finding work after testifying to the Rogers Commission.

is no longer as confident of its technological capabilities as it was in the 1960s and no longer takes pride in space exploration.

CHAPTER 3 **Personal Narratives**

before the other channels could break into their programming.

FOREWORD

"History cannot give us a program for the future, but it can give us a fuller understanding of ourselves, and of our common humanity, so that we can better face the future."
— *Robert Penn Warren,*
American poet and novelist

The history of each nation is punctuated by momentous events that represent turning points for that nation, with an impact felt far beyond its borders. These events—displaying the full range of human capabilities, from violence, greed, and ignorance to heroism, courage, and strength—are nearly always complicated and multifaceted. Any student of history faces the challenge of grasping the many strands that constitute such world-changing events as wars, social movements, and environmental disasters. But understanding these significant historic events can be enhanced by exposure to a variety of perspectives, whether of people involved intimately or of ones observing from a distance of miles or years. Understanding can also be increased by learning about the controversies surrounding such events and exploring hot-button issues from multiple angles. Finally, true understanding of important historic events involves knowledge of the events' human impact—of the ways such events affected people in their everyday lives—all over the world.

Perspectives on Modern World History examines global historic events from the twentieth-century onward by presenting analysis and observation from numerous vantage points. Each volume offers high school, early college level, and general interest readers a thematically arranged anthology of previously published materials that address a major historical event, with an emphasis on international coverage. Each volume opens with background information on the event, then presents the controversies surrounding that event, and concludes with first-person narratives from people who lived through the event or were affected by it. By providing primary sources from the time of the event, as well as relevant commentary surrounding the event, this series can be used to inform debate, help develop critical thinking skills, increase global awareness, and enhance an understanding of international perspectives on history.

Material in each volume is selected from a diverse range of sources, including journals, magazines, newspapers, nonfiction books, personal narratives, speeches, congressional testimony, government documents, pamphlets, organization newsletters, and position papers. Articles taken from these sources are carefully edited and introduced to provide context and background. Each volume of Perspectives on Modern World History includes an array of views on events of global significance. Much of the material comes from international sources and from U.S. sources that provide extensive international coverage.

Each volume in the Perspectives on Modern World History series also includes:

- A full-color **world map**, offering context and geographic perspective.
- An annotated **table of contents** that provides a brief summary of each essay in the volume.
- An **introduction** specific to the volume topic.
- For each viewpoint, a brief **introduction** that has notes about the author and source of the viewpoint, and that provides a summary of its main points.
- Full-color **charts**, **graphs**, **maps**, and other visual representations.

- Informational **sidebars** that explore the lives of key individuals, give background on historical events, or explain scientific or technical concepts.
- A **glossary** that defines key terms, as needed.
- A **chronology** of important dates preceding, during, and immediately following the event.
- A **bibliography** of additional books, periodicals, and Web sites for further research.
- A comprehensive **subject index** that offers access to people, places, and events cited in the text.

Perspectives on Modern World History is designed for a broad spectrum of readers who want to learn more about not only history but also current events, political science, government, international relations, and sociology—students doing research for class assignments or debates, teachers and faculty seeking to supplement course materials, and others wanting to improve their understanding of history. Each volume of Perspectives on Modern World History is designed to illuminate a complicated event, to spark debate, and to show the human perspective behind the world's most significant happenings of recent decades.

INTRODUCTION

The morning of January 28, 1986, was exceptionally cold in Florida, where freezing weather is rare. The beaches near the Kennedy Space Center were crowded with people who had come to watch the launch of the space shuttle *Challenger*, which had been postponed on several preceding days to great disappointment. Although shuttle launches were considered so routine that network television no longer broadcast them, there was special interest in this one because a teacher—the first private citizen to go into space—was on board. Christa McAuliffe, a high school social studies teacher from Concord, New Hampshire, had been chosen from among eleven thousand applicants and was scheduled to teach several lessons during the flight. Students at all grade levels were looking forward to them, and busloads of children had been brought to the viewing area to see the launch, along with many others who were watching from their classrooms via closed-circuit television.

Like all space launches, this one was spectacular—the ship rose on a roaring tower of flame, and bright rockets arced into a clear blue sky. But then something horrifying happened. Seventy-three seconds after liftoff, the rockets' white vapor trail burst into huge billowing plumes branching off at odd angles. People who had observed previous launches were puzzled, but cheering from the crowd continued until it was abruptly silenced by an announcement over the loudspeakers: "Obviously a major malfunction"—and, after a pause, "we have a report from the Flight Dynamics Officer that the vehicle has exploded."

Later, experts learned that the *Challenger* had not exploded, although most media continued to say that it had; actually it disintegrated due to aerodynamic forces after a fire—caused by the cold weather's effect on a poorly-designed joint seal that damaged one of the solid rocket boosters. But from below, it looked like an explosion, and the outcome was equivalent. All seven members of the crew were killed.

These were the first deaths to occur during a US space flight. Three astronauts had died by fire nineteen years earlier in a capsule test on the ground, but there had been nearly twenty-five years of space flight, fifty-five US missions in a row, without a single in-flight fatality—an almost miraculous record. The public, unlike the astronauts and others knowledgeable about space technology, had come to believe that going into space was safe. And so people reacted not only with grief, but with shock. The nation and much of the world was stunned by the accident. Children who saw it on live TV were devastated. For days—and in some cases years—afterward, many Americans were deeply upset, far beyond the sorrow felt for victims of other disasters.

Some, once they grasped the fact that space flight is inherently risky, began to say that such risks should not be taken. Others were surprised by this reaction. Why, they wondered, was it different from the widely accepted risks of aviation, a field that cost countless lives in its early years and is still subject to frequent well-publicized crashes? Explorers have always risked their lives. For that matter, people risk their lives in dangerous sports, and death on the highway is a possibility accepted regularly by everyone who drives. Why should it have been thought that space travel, unlike any other potentially fatal activity in human history, would be blessed forever with freedom from everyday harsh reality?

One possible answer was posted the day after the disaster on a Portland, Oregon, BBS (a local electronic bulletin board popular in the era before the Internet). The writer suggested that to many people, space wasn't part of reality. "They seem to think that, like a television show with good guys and bad guys, everything will come out well in the end and good will always triumph over evil," she wrote. "They reacted with shock and horror, perhaps partly because the space program wasn't real to them. After all, the good guys always survive."

Perhaps to some Americans, space ventures were no more real than TV shows such as *Star Trek*. Many people enjoyed *Star Trek* and other science fiction, because it said something, albeit not very literally, about the real future. Had others enjoyed real space launches because they made life seem like a fantasy world? Quite a few bloggers on the Internet, looking back on their childhood, have said that viewing the *Challenger* accident was the moment when they first became aware of death. Perhaps that disillusionment was among the reasons why interest in space began to gradually decline after the accident. A few days after the disaster, polls showed that about 80 percent of the public supported continuation of manned space flights; but the next year, the percentage was smaller. While polls still show a majority in favor of manned space flights, few have pushed for funding. As of 2012, no more NASA manned flights are scheduled.

There were other factors contributing to the impact of *Challenger*'s loss on the public. On the twenty-sixth anniversary of the disaster, an editorial in the North Carolina newspaper *Mount Airy News* summed up a view that is often expressed throughout the United States: "I think when that shuttle flight ended, when McAuliffe and the other astronauts died . . . something was lost in our nation. Space was no longer the final frontier, something to be explored and tamed. It became a dangerous place, empty, and the value of exploring it became an empty promise that couldn't possibly live up to the danger or expense." To those who believe that becoming a spacefaring species is of vital importance to the human race, this is a more far-reaching tragedy than the loss of the crew, from the astronauts' standpoint as well as humankind's.

Heroes have died in achieving every advance humans have ever made. They have risked their lives in the belief that even their death would further the goal to which they were committed. For it to have the opposite effect—for their sacrifice to lead to abandonment of the goal—would be the worst thing imaginable to such men and women, were they alive to see it happen. Over the years, astronauts have frequently declared that they would not want space flight to stop if they were killed in an accident. So for many people, grief for the Challenger Seven was magnified by the fear that they might have died in vain.

To some people, the costs and risks of manned space flight are not warranted. In the eyes of these people, the promise of space was created by media hype, and loss of faith in it was not a matter for regret. Furthermore, the shuttle program had critics even among ardent space supporters, for unlike the United States' earlier space efforts, it did not appear to have a well-defined aim. So whether this particular flight was worth seven lives is open to question, especially because its chief practical purpose was merely to place a commercial satellite in orbit.

But in the view of many, the meaning of space missions extends beyond their immediate practical value. Dick Scobee, *Challenger*'s commander, told a journalist,

> My perception is the real significance of [this flight], and especially a teacher, is that it will get people in this country, especially the young people, expecting to fly in space. . . . The short-term gain is a publicity gain. The long term gain is getting expectations of the young people in this country to the point where they expect to fly in space, they expect to go there, they expect this country to pursue a program that allows it to be in

space permanently to work and live there, to explore the planets.

Though the *Challenger* disaster is not the only reason the majority of young people feel less enthusiasm for space today than they did several generations ago, it undoubtedly contributed to the fading of that enthusiasm. In the 1960s and 1970s, anything connected with space fascinated kids. Even in the 1980s, many children wished to become astronauts. On a national newscast following the *Challenger* disaster, one child said that he had always wanted to be an astronaut but had changed his mind. Judging by the apathy toward space exploration felt by today's children and teens, that boy spoke for many.

In a speech upon receiving the Challenger Center Presidential Award in 1995, former president George H.W. Bush said:

> Never before in our nation's history has America surveyed a frontier and then retreated. We have always been a people among whose basic urges is to seek out the distant horizon, to surpass it, to go to the next, and the next after that. . . . It is the stuff of our history—the stuff of our past. I believe it should also have a place in our future.
>
> The Challenger Seven lived in vibrant pursuit of a dream. As long as we continue to pursue that dream, as long as we help it to touch the lives of our young people, as long as we help to ensure that America continues to rise to the challenge of the new frontier, then it can be said that we never truly lost those seven brave souls. They will continue to live on with us, and with the hopes and dreams of the nation.

Such hopes and dreams are shared by many around the world, for the belief that humankind will someday venture farther into space is by no means confined to the United States. Despite the controversies surrounding the space shuttle program and manned space flight in general, the men and women aboard *Challenger* had a vision that will endure.

Perspectives on Modern World History: The Challenger Disaster examines the cause of the shuttle accident, its impact on society, and its long-term effect on US space exploration.

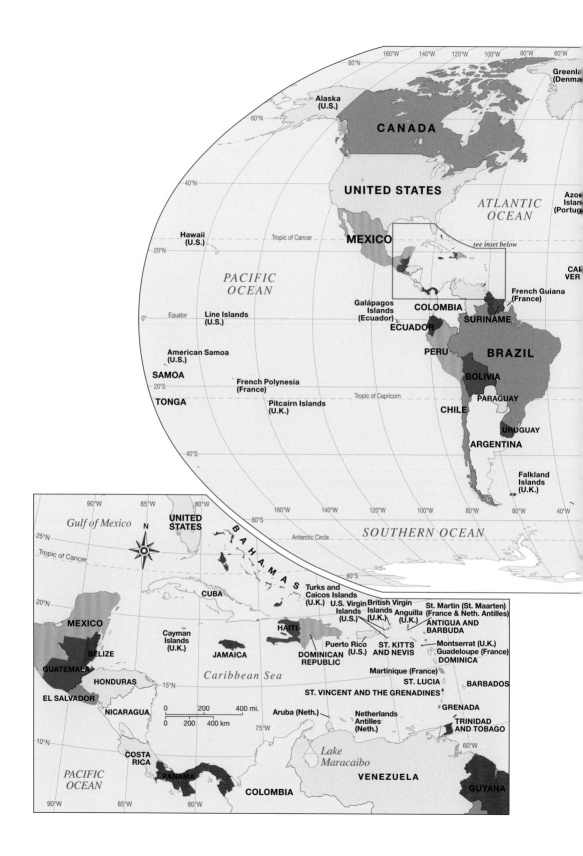

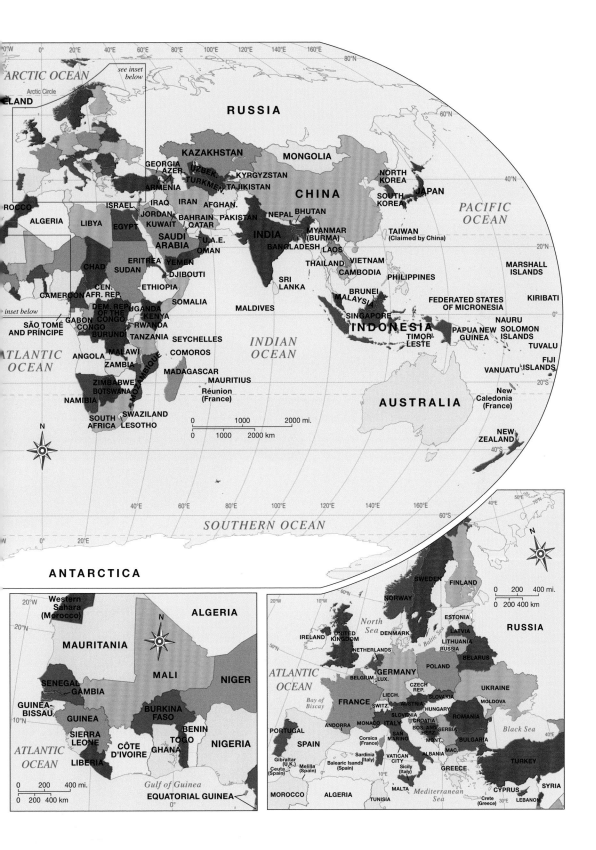

CHAPTER 1

Historical Background on the *Challenger* Disaster

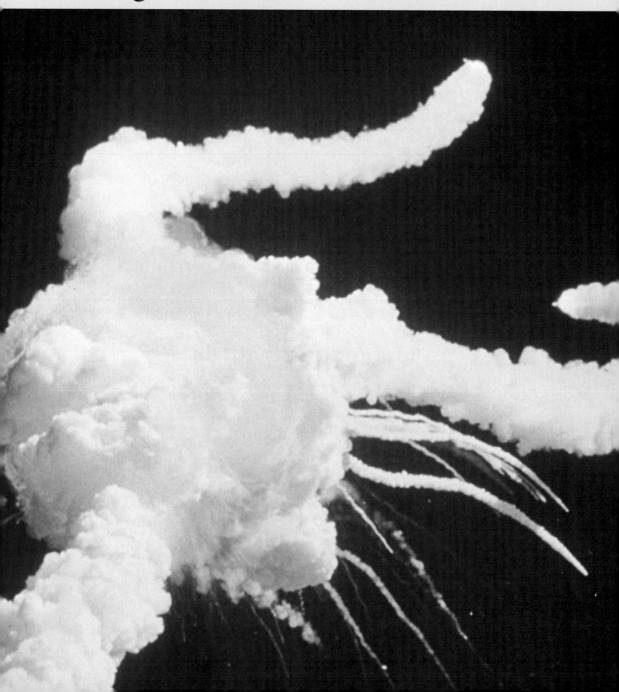

An Overview of the *Challenger* Disaster

Jennifer Rosenberg

In the following viewpoint, a historian details the *Challenger* accident. On January 28, 1986, the space shuttle *Challenger* broke apart seventy-three seconds after liftoff, and the seven members of the crew were killed. Among them was Christa McAuliffe, a teacher and the first private citizen in space. These were the first American deaths in space, and the nation reacted with shock. A presidential commission was established to determine what had gone wrong. The author explains the cause of the failure, which involved the effect of extreme cold weather on the O-rings that sealed pieces of the rocket together and the later discovery that at least some of the crew members had been alive when the cabin hit the ocean. Jennifer Rosenberg is a historian and writer.

Photo on previous page: The *Challenger* space shuttle broke up in mid-air seconds after liftoff, killing all seven crew members on board, on January 28, 1986. It was the worst tragedy to date in NASA's history. (© **Michele McDonald/Virginian-Pilot/AP Images.**)

Around 8:30 A.M. on Tuesday, January 28, 1986, in Florida, the seven crew members of the Space Shuttle *Challenger* were already strapped into

SOURCE. Jennifer Rosenberg, "Space Shuttle Challenger Disaster," About.com. http://history1900s.about.com. © 2013 Jennifer Rosenberg. Used with permission of About Inc., which can be found online at www.about.com. All rights reserved.

their seats. Though they were ready to go, NASA officials were busy deciding whether it was safe enough to launch that day. It had been extremely cold the night before, causing icicles to form under the launch pad. By morning, temperatures were still only 32°F (0°C). If the shuttle launched that day, it would be the coldest day of any shuttle launch.

Safety was a huge concern, but NASA officials were also under pressure to get the shuttle into orbit quickly. Weather and malfunctions had already caused many postponements from the original launch date, January 22. If the shuttle didn't launch by February 1, some of the science experiments and business arrangements regarding the satellite would be jeopardized. Plus, millions of people, especially students across the U.S., were waiting and watching for this particular mission to launch.

Among the crew on board the *Challenger* that morning was Sharon "Christa" McAuliffe. McAuliffe, a social studies teacher at Concord High School in New Hampshire, had been chosen from 11,000 applicants to participate in the Teacher in Space Project. President Ronald Reagan created this project in August 1984 in an effort to increase public interest in the U.S. space program. The teacher chosen would become the first private citizen in space.

A teacher, a wife, and a mother of two, McAuliffe represented the average, good-natured citizen. She became the face of NASA for nearly a year before the launch and the public adored her.

A little after 11:00 A.M. on that cold morning, NASA told the crew that launch was a go. At 11:38 A.M., the Space Shuttle *Challenger* launched from Pad 39-B at the Kennedy Space Center at Cape Canaveral, Florida.

At first, everything seemed to go well. However, 73 seconds after lift-off, Mission Control heard Pilot Mike Smith say, "Uh oh!" Then people at Mission Control,

Photo on previous page: The *Challenger* space shuttle takes off early in the morning of January 28, 1986. (© NASA/AP Images.)

observers on the ground, and millions of children and adults across the nation watched as the Space Shuttle *Challenger* exploded.

The nation was shocked. To this day, many remember exactly where they were and what they were doing when they heard that the *Challenger* had exploded. It remains a defining moment in the 20th century.

An hour after the explosion, search and recovery planes and ships searched for survivors and wreckage. Though some pieces of the shuttle floated on the surface of the Atlantic Ocean, much of it had sunk to the bottom. No survivors were found. On January 31, 1986, three days after the disaster, a memorial service was held for the fallen heroes.

> "To this day, many remember exactly where they were and what they were doing when they heard that the *Challenger* had exploded."

What Went Wrong

Everyone wanted to know what had gone wrong. On February 3, 1986, President Reagan established the Presidential Commission on the Space Shuttle Challenger Accident. Former Secretary of State William Rogers chaired the commission, whose members included [astronauts] Sally Ride, Neil Armstrong, and Chuck Yeager. The "Rogers Commission" carefully studied pictures, video, and debris from the accident. The Commission determined that the accident was caused by a failure in the O-rings of the right solid rocket booster.

O-rings sealed the pieces of the rocket booster together. From multiple uses and especially because of the extreme cold on that day, an O-ring on the right rocket booster had become brittle. Once launched, the weak O-ring allowed fire to escape from the rocket booster. The fire melted a support beam that held the booster

The *Challenger* Did Not Explode

Contrary to the flight dynamics officer's initial statement, the shuttle and external tank did not actually "explode." Instead they rapidly disintegrated under tremendous aerodynamic forces, since the shuttle was past "Max Q," or maximum aerodynamic pressure. When the external tank disintegrated, the fuel and oxidizer stored within it were released, producing the appearance of a massive fireball. However, according to the NASA team that analyzed imagery after the accident, there was only "localized combustion" of propellant. Instead, the visible cloud was primarily composed of vapor and gases resulting from the release of the shuttle's liquid oxygen and liquid hydrogen propellant. Stored in cryogenic conditions, the liquid hydrogen could not have ignited rapidly enough to trigger an "explosion" in the traditional sense of a detonation (as opposed to a deflagration, which was what occurred). Had there been a true explosion, the entire shuttle would have been instantly destroyed, killing the crew at that moment. The more robustly constructed crew cabin and SRBs [solid rocket boosters] survived the breakup of the launch vehicle; while the SRBs were subsequently detonated remotely, the detached cabin continued along a ballistic trajectory, and was observed exiting the cloud of gases at T+75.237. Twenty-five seconds after the breakup of the vehicle, which occurred at 48,000 feet (14.6 km), the trajectory of the crew compartment peaked at a height of 65,000 feet (19.8 km).

SOURCE. "Challenger," *New Zealand Safety Council, 2008. www.safetycouncil .org.*

in place. The booster, then mobile, hit the fuel tank, causing the explosion. Upon further research, it was determined that there had been multiple, unheeded warnings about the potential problems with the O-rings.

On March 8, 1986, a search team found the crew cabin; it had not been destroyed in the explosion. The bodies of all seven crew members were found, still strapped into their seats. Autopsies were done but exact cause of death was inconclusive. It is believed that at least some of the crew survived the explosion, since three of four emergency air packs found had been deployed. After the explosion, the crew cabin fell over 50,000 feet and hit the water at approximately 200 miles per hour. None could have survived the impact.

A Florida Newspaper Reports on the *Challenger* Disaster

James Fisher

In the following viewpoint, a journalist reports on the *Challenger* disaster and the reactions throughout the nation a day after the accident. No one yet knew the cause of the accident, and NASA said that a review of data from the flight would be conducted. It maintained that despite the previous days' cancellations, there had been no pressure to launch, and flight safety had been the top priority in the decision. Vice President George H.W. Bush arrived at the Kennedy Space Center late in the afternoon to offer condolences to the crew members' families, who had watched the launch. Meanwhile, a recovery force had been sent to search for debris in the ocean. The TV networks had not carried the launch live, the author says, but broke into their programming to broadcast replays. James Fisher was a reporter for the *Orlando Sentinel* at the time of the *Challenger* disaster.

SOURCE. James Fisher, "Coverage from the Day Space Shuttle Challenger Exploded: What Went Wrong?," *Orlando Sentinel*, January 29, 1986. Copyright © 1986 by Orlando Sentinel. All rights reserved. Reproduced by permission.

Grief, investigations and soul-searching shrouded America's troubled shuttle program Tuesday [January 28, 1986] after the catastrophic explosion of *Challenger* that took seven lives—the greatest tragedy in man's conquest of space.

"We mourn seven heroes," said President [Ronald] Reagan.

As students around the nation watched on television, schoolteacher Christa McAuliffe and six astronauts perished in a huge fireball when it was 10 miles high and 8 miles south-southeast of Cape Canaveral at 11:39 A.M., 75 seconds after launch.

It was the first time American astronauts died in flight, and the worst U.S. space tragedy since Gus Grissom, Ed White and Roger Chaffee died in an Apollo spacecraft fire during a mock countdown Jan. 27, 1967.

Victims of America's 56th manned spaceflight, the 25th of the shuttle program and *Challenger*'s 10th were commander Francis "Dick" Scobee, 46, pilot Michael Smith, 40, Judith Resnik, 36, Ellison Onizuka, 39, Ronald McNair, 35, engineer Gregory Jarvis, 41, and McAuliffe, 37, the Concord, N.H., social studies teacher chosen from 11,000 applicants to be the first private citizen in space.

Many of their families, including McAuliffe's, watched in horror from nearby sites several miles from refurbished launch pad 39B, used for the first time since 1975.

Hours later, heat-resistant shuttle tiles began washing ashore south of the Cape. Passers-by were taking them to the south gate of the Cape, where they were being driven to the Kennedy Space Center.

Col. Bob Nicholson, an Air Force spokesman, said every available piece of debris would be needed for the investigation. But he said some debris could contain explosives, and for people to call the Air Force if there is any question about the nature of the debris.

Rescue craft were retrieving other debris, mostly tiles.

Stunned NASA officials refused to speculate on what went wrong, but it appeared trouble could have developed in the huge external fuel tank, launched with 528,000 gallons of volatile liquid propellants.

The 2,200-ton spaceplane, whose boosters carried 2.2 million pounds of solid propellant, lifted off normally at 11:38 A.M. Then the boosters ejected sideways as *Challenger* and the external tank exploded.

> "The boosters spiraled away, spinning like skyrockets . . . as they careened toward the Atlantic far below. "

The boosters spiraled away, spinning like skyrockets with flames gushing from their nozzles as they careened toward the Atlantic far below.

There was no sign of life.

The Cause of the Accident Was Unknown

Television pictures indicated the explosion might have originated in the shuttle's external tank.

"We will not speculate as to the specific cause of the explosion based on that footage," said NASA shuttle chief Jesse Moore. "It will take all the data, a careful review of that data before we can draw any conclusions on this national tragedy."

He said the space agency is forming an investigating board that will make a "careful review" of all data "before we can reach any conclusions." Two congressional committees announced investigations.

Moore said he had created an interim investigative board "to implement preliminary activities in this tragedy," to secure all data so it can be fully analyzed.

NASA acting Administrator William Graham will appoint an official investigation board within a day or two, Moore said.

"Data from all the shuttle instrumentation, photographs, launch pad systems, hardware, cargo, ground support systems and even notes made by any member of the launch team and flight operations team are being impounded for study."

"There were no signs of abnormalities on the screens" as flight controllers monitored *Challenger's* liftoff and ascent, said an official at the Johnson Space Center in Houston. He said the blast came "unexpectedly and with absolutely no warning."

The shuttle's three main engines had just returned to full power after they had been cut to 65 percent power to reduce stress from gravity and other forces in the first minute of launch.

"We have a major malfunction," came a voice over the loudspeaker.

Seconds later a spokesman in Mission Control in Houston said:

"We have a report from the flight dynamics officer that the vehicle has exploded. The flight director confirms that. We are checking with the recovery forces to see what can be done at this point."

Jess Parrish Memorial Hospital in Titusville, [Florida,] the first stop for injured astronauts, never was put on alert. Within five minutes of the explosion, NASA "informed us they wouldn't need us," said hospital administrator Richard Lind.

The impact area is about 60 by 120 miles, beginning about 50 miles southeast of the launch pad, said Air Force Col. Nicholson. The area is centered about 18 miles south-southeast of Cape Canaveral.

Recovery ships and aircraft were prevented from entering the recovery area for almost an hour afterward because radar indicated debris was still falling, Nicholson said.

The purpose of the mission was to release and retrieve one satellite to study Halley's Comet and launch another to become part of the space-based shuttle communications network.

The insignia for *Challenger* mission STS-51-L included a small apple next to teacher Christa McAuliffe's name, signifying the mission's educational agenda. (© **Corbis.**)

McAuliffe Wasn't Worried About Safety

McAuliffe was to teach two 15-minute lessons on the fourth day of the mission. Public Broadcasting Service was to carry the telecast live, and hundreds of schools planned to tune in.

Linda Long, who had been an aide to McAuliffe since last September, said the teacher had confidence in NASA and the shuttle program and wasn't worried about her safety.

"What she told me some time ago was that she anticipated the flight almost like the way you anticipate riding a roller coaster," Long said.

Tuesday morning, Long told McAuliffe she thought the shuttle would lift off.

"She said 'great.' She turned around and smiled. She was ready to go."

Among those who witnessed the explosion were McAuliffe's attorney-husband Steve and their two children, Scott, 9, and Caroline, 6. Also on hand were members of Scott's third-grade class from Concord, N.H., displaying a large "Go Christa" banner.

McAuliffe's parents, Ed and Grace Corrigan, of Framingham, Mass., stood silently during the launch, arm in arm. A NASA official climbed up rows into the bleachers, walked to them and said, "The vehicle has exploded."

Mrs. Corrigan looked back at him. "The vehicle has exploded?" she asked. He nodded silently and the Corrigans were quickly led away.

All 1,200 students at McAuliffe's Concord High School were cheering the televised launch when a teacher yelled for them to be silent because something appeared to be wrong.

NASA Suspends the Shuttle Program

The U.S. House interrupted its session and the chaplain delivered a prayer for the astronauts. The House then adjourned.

The flag at Kennedy Space Center rested at half-staff after the explosion.

"There was absolutely no pressure to get this particular launch off," Moore said.

"We have always maintained that flight safety is our top priority. All of the people involved in the program, to my knowledge, thought that *Challenger* was quite ready to go, and I made the decision along with the . . . support team that we launch."

Moore said he has suspended operation of the shuttle program "for a few days so we can sit down and assess this. We are not going to pick up any flight activity until we fully understand what the circumstances are."

When launches will resume "is very difficult to estimate at this time. It's going to be a function of what the board finds were the difficulties today and what corrective actions have to be taken," he said.

Rockwell International, the shuttle manufacturer, is continuing to build shuttle spare parts and could supply another shuttle if NASA and the government decide to get another, Moore said.

He said the shuttle program did not necessarily have to have four shuttles to meet its goals.

Asked if the shuttle is too complex to be reliable, Moore said, "I don't want to speculate on that at this point in time. It will be a logical question for somebody to ask."

FBI spokesman Gary Bray in Orlando said several agents from Orlando and Cocoa were sent to the Kennedy center to work with NASA investigators on the cause of the tragedy.

"We're over there investigating if there was any possible act of sabotage involved," Bray said.

Bray said there was no evidence of sabotage but an investigation will be conducted to see if there was any act of willful negligence by NASA employees or subcontract employees who worked on the shuttle.

Vice President George Bush, Ohio Sen. John Glenn—an early astronaut—and Utah Sen. Jake Garn, who flew on the shuttle last April, arrived at Kennedy Space Center about 6 P.M. to offer their condolences to the victims' families.

To schoolchildren, Bush said, "You must try to understand that spirit, bravery and commitment are what make not only the space program, but all of life worthwhile.

"We must never . . . stop hoping, stop exploring or stop discovering."

Glenn said, "In nearly a quarter of a century, we thought this might happen sometime, but we delayed that day until today."

> 'In nearly a quarter of a century, we thought this might happen sometime, but we delayed that day until today.'

The *Challenger*'s crew (from left): Teacher in Space participant Sharon Christa McAuliffe, payload specialist Greg Jarvis, mission specialist Judy Resnik, commander Dick Scobee, mission specialist Ron McNair, pilot Mike Smith, and mission specialist Ellison S. Onizuka. All seven perished. (© **Photo 12/ Universal Images Group/ Getty Images.**)

"While we have many triumphs, many of them, once in a while there is tragedy," said Glenn, the first American to orbit Earth.

The immediate families of the seven crew members watched the launch from atop the launch control center. Parents and other relatives watched from the VIP bleachers near the press site about two blocks away.

Recovery of Debris Will Continue

The recovery force included two C-130 Coast Guard planes, two Patrick Air Force Base H-3 Jolly Green Giant helicopters, the solid rocket booster recovery ship *Liberty*, a Coast Guard hydrofoil boat, two Navy H-3 helicopters, and a Coast Guard cutter from Grand Bahamas Island. Later other ships joined the search.

A scallop boat owner offered the use of his fleet and possibly other fleets in the search, but officials declined because of the possibility of live explosives in the area, Nicholson said.

At first the rescue operation was overseen by the office of the commander of the Atlantic Fleet in Norfolk,

Va. One of the Patrick Jolly Green copters was in charge at the scene.

Later the Coast Guard in Miami took charge.

A parachute was attached to one piece of debris, possibly from one of the rocket boosters.

The water in the recovery area is about 120 feet deep.

Aircraft crews were pointing out debris for the ships to pick up, but at one point low clouds made visibility too poor for the aircraft to be much help.

The planes had to give up the search because of darkness Tuesday evening, but the ships were expected to stay in the area.

The launch, postponed six times because of weather and problems with the previous *Columbia* mission, had been set for 9:38 A.M. But replacement of some launch pad circuitry overnight related to the fire extinguisher system delayed it an hour. It was further delayed to allow for inspection for ice Tuesday morning.

When liftoff occurred, the sky was perfectly clear.

Challenger was considered the workhorse of NASA's shuttle fleet.

The fiery explosion, including the separation of the boosters, could be seen plainly from as far away as Tampa, witnesses reported.

President Reagan watched tape replays in "stunned silence," and postponed the State of the Union message he was to deliver Tuesday night. He made an evening Oval Office speech on the tragedy and sent Bush to Florida to convey his sympathies to the families of the crew members.

> Americans everywhere watched in disbelief as television networks replayed the shuttle explosion.

Americans everywhere watched in disbelief as television networks replayed the shuttle explosion.

Ironically, launches have become so routine that the major TV networks did not show this one live, and had to break into regular programming once the tragedy was clear. Cable News Network [CNN] and many public television stations did broadcast live, and viewers saw the routine turn into disaster.

NASA administrator Graham was briefing members of Congress on the agency budget and watched the tragedy on television. Two members who had flown recent missions, Garn and Rep. Bill Nelson, D-Melbourne, expressed shock.

The Tuesday launch was to be the second of 15 this year—by far the most ambitious schedule in NASA's four-year shuttle program. Garn said the obvious—that operations must be frozen for as long as it takes NASA to investigate and understand what went wrong.

Half an hour after the explosion, a wisp of white smoke, blown by upper winds, still marked the path of the shuttle's wreckage.

Observers React with Shock to the Destruction of *Challenger*

Kathy Sawyer

In the following viewpoint, a journalist describes the launch of *Challenger*, at which she was present, telling how long it took for the disbelieving crowd to grasp the fact that the crew had been lost. Many people were crying, she reports. The editor of the student newspaper at the high school where Christa McAuliffe taught said he felt sick, and McAuliffe's parents were in shock, as was the teacher who had been her backup. The author recalls how happy and excited the crew had seemed earlier in the morning when they appeared to the crowd on the closed-circuit television monitors, and how McAuliffe had said in the past that she thought of herself as a pioneer. Kathy Sawyer was a *Washington Post* staff writer at the time of the *Challenger* disaster.

Awareness came slowly, not in a fiery burst, to those watching the shuttle launch from the better seats—the grandstands set up for families of

---

SOURCE. Kathy Sawyer, "The Horror Dawned Slowly," *Washington Post*, January 29, 1986. Copyright © 1986 by the Washington Post. All rights reserved. Reproduced by permission.

the astronauts, dignitaries, the news media and a class of third graders with connections.

The chest-trembling, concussive roar of the liftoff, lagging behind the rising spaceship, had reached us. The spacecraft, clinging fly-fashion to the "wall" of tanks containing 3.8 million pounds of fuel, had been up about one minute.

We were gasping and cheering at the column of fire-topped smoke growing like a beanstalk into a cold, blue sky. As the rumbling sound (still trailing the visible scene) continued, a curious rooster tail seemed to form almost gently at the top, with glints of fire in it.

It took an age to realize that the column ended there.

One of the smaller solid rocket boosters could be seen looping out and back in toward the shuttle, trailing smoke. Other trails appeared.

The Horror Dawns Slowly

"Obviously . . . a major malfunction . . . has occurred," the voice of Mission Control, Steve Nesbitt, who normally speaks crisply, said slowly over the NASA public address system.

"They're coming back," said *Reader's Digest* writer Malcolm McConnell, who has covered 10 launches. He and several other reporters started running, planning to make their way to the landing strip several miles away where the shuttle was to return in an emergency. There were confused shouts, swearing, a short scream.

Then, still looking up, McConnell sat back down. "Where are they?" someone asked. "Dead," he answered flatly. "We've lost 'em, God bless 'em."

Phrases drifted down from Mission Control. ". . . Appeared nominal through engine throttles back . . . apparent explosion. . . . Tracking crews have reported that the vehicle had exploded."

Shortly, there was the announcement that an "impact point" had been located in the ocean.

Christa McAuliffe's family—(left to right) sister Betsy, and parents Grace and Ed Corrigan—realize that the *Challenger* has blown apart in mid-air during lift off as they watched from the Kennedy Space Center. (© **Jim Cole/ AP Images.**)

The rumbling sounds from the sky gradually died away. The scattered screams and shouts died. The immediate families of the astronauts were escorted quickly away to the crew quarters. Other relatives and visitors were urged onto the buses that had brought them to the scene.

Then this stretch of Kennedy Space Center along an Atlantic Ocean beach was overwhelmed in silence.

The beanstalk of cloud, ending in a large blossom, hung in the air for hours, breaking lazily into smaller puffs. The debris from the explosion, which occurred 18 miles downrange from the space center, continued to fall into the ocean for nearly an hour, the loudspeaker voice explained later, and thwarted the search teams on helicopters, planes and ships that were converging on the spot.

The closed-circuit television monitors scattered everywhere in the press area, which had recorded the bustle of launch activity, the suiting up of the astronauts, one by one, now showed an empty picture of Atlantic horizon.

> Some . . . compared their feelings to the aftershock of combat, others to the day President John F. Kennedy was shot.

Some of the crustier observers here compared their feelings to the aftershock of combat, others to the day President John F. Kennedy was shot.

Some people sobbed. Most had red eyes.

Teacher's Students and Family View the Explosion

"I was just standing, looking up, watching for the shuttle to come out of the cloud," said Brian Ballard, 16, editor of a student newspaper.

Christa McAuliffe, 37, a social studies teacher from his school, Concord High in Concord, N.H., was in the middeck section of the spacecraft, part of the seven-member crew. She had been officially designated by the White House as the "first private citizen in space." Officials had hoped her participation would rekindle interest in the space program among schoolchildren.

"My stomach turned over," Ballard said quietly a little while after the explosion, recalling the moment of realization. "I felt sick right that minute."

McAuliffe's parents and other relatives were standing in the VIP grandstand area surrounded by a white picket fence, a parking lot between them and the press stands. They were with the visiting third-grade class of about 20 children that had traveled here with McAuliffe's son, Scott, 9, last week. Scott, McAuliffe's daughter, Caroline, 6, and the teacher's husband, Steven, were

The Crew of *Challenger*

Francis R. "Dick" Scobee, the spacecraft commander, was a commander in the US Air Force and a former Air Force test pilot. He had been the pilot of *Challenger*'s fifth orbital flight in 1974.

Michael J. Smith, the pilot, was a commander in the US Navy who had been a Navy test pilot. This was his first space flight.

Judith A. Resnik, a mission specialist, had a PhD in electrical engineering. She had become the second woman astronaut in orbit, and the first American Jew, when she flew on *Discovery* in 1984.

Ronald E. McNair, a mission specialist, had a PhD in physics. He was enthusiastic about athletics and had a black belt in karate. He had become the second black American in orbit on a previous *Challenger* flight.

Ellison Onizuka, a mission specialist, was a Japanese-American born in Hawaii. He had served as an Air Force aerospace flight test engineer and later as chief of the engineering support section at Edwards Air Force Base. This was his second shuttle mission.

Gregory B. Jarvis, a payload specialist, was an employee of Hughes Aircraft Company who had competed against six hundred other Hughes employees for sponsorship as an astronaut. His duties concerned gathering data related to rocket design.

watching from the roof of the nearby Launch Control Center, at the foot of the giant Vehicle Assembly Building. The grandstands are 3½ miles from the launching pad—as close as it is safe to get, officials here said, to the rockets' potentially explosive 3.8 million pounds of fuel at liftoff.

Bob Hohler, a reporter for the *Concord Monitor*, had followed McAuliffe for seven months, from the time she became a finalist in the competition for yesterday's [January 28, 1986] brief ride.

At liftoff, he was watching McAuliffe's parents, Edward and Grace Corrigan, through a telephoto camera lens.

"They already had tears in their eyes, from the liftoff," he said. "As the truth of what had happened dawned on them, they kept looking up, the tears of delight still on their faces, their mouths half-open. I guess they were in shock."

Then a man standing nearby put his hand on Edward Corrigan's arm and led him and his wife away. Someone else was calling "Back to the buses, please get on the buses," to the other visitors.

A NASA official who was with McAuliffe's parents during the launch said afterward, "I'll never forget the expression on her mother's face."

Barbara Morgan, the teacher chosen as backup to McAuliffe, had stood on a TV platform near the press stand. Just at ignition and liftoff, she had smiled and waved, "Bye, Christa. Bye, Christa."

A minute later she was being helped from the platform, shaken.

A grizzled senior Lockheed technician who helped close out the shuttle before launch sat tiredly drinking a cup of coffee in the NASA cafeteria $1\frac{1}{2}$ hours after the disaster.

> The launch had attracted dozens of busloads of schoolchildren and their teachers, to see the 'teacher in space.'

"I stood in that field watching them, and I saw the Lord took 'em in a twinkling," he said. "I don't feel sorry for those brave people because they're with the Lord. I feel sorry for the children."

The launch had attracted dozens of busloads of schoolchildren and their teachers, to see the "teacher in space." On the mission's fourth day, McAuliffe had planned to teach the first classes from space, beginning with one entitled "The Ultimate Field Trip."

Freezing Weather for the Launch

The morning activities had begun before dawn in high, if chilly spirits. After six delays, it looked as if the mission would finally go up.

Watching the closed-circuit monitors, we had followed the preparations on the launch pad. One by one, the proud and smiling members of the crew appeared in the "White Room," the enclosed entryway attached to the *Challenger*'s hatch, and put the final touches on their spacesuits.

The room got unusually crowded because everyone was pushing in to get out of the below-freezing weather.

A member of the supporting crew, who had come to be known in Mission Control reports as Sonny (Billy Bob) Carter, gave the space teacher an apple as she appeared in the "White Room," welcoming her as a special passenger. (Before the previous day's launch had been scrubbed, Carter had welcomed her wearing a mortarboard with tassel.) Even on the closed-circuit screens, she seemed to glow with delight.

McAuliffe was the first to climb into an American spacecraft with no special training in science or aeronautics, other than the 400 hours' worth that followed her selection from among 11,000 teacher-applicants. After some smiles and small talk with other crew members, she put a little white cap on her dark curls, and then the massive space helmet.

She is reported to have said, "I really feel a part of this crew."

At 8:35 A.M., Christa McAuliffe crawled through the Challenger hatch, her foot disappearing last.

The other woman on board, Judith A. Resnik, 36, was one of the four astronauts on the flight crew who had already taken shuttle flights. She was an electrical and biomedical engineer. The other veterans included Francis R. (Dick) Scobee, 46, the spacecraft commander who had logged more than 6,500 hours in 45 types of aircraft;

Air Force Lt. Col. Ellison S. Onizuka, 39, and Ronald E. McNair, 35, a physicist.

Rookie astronaut Michael J. Smith, 40, a Navy Commander, was the pilot. Engineer Gregory B. Jarvis, 41, of Hughes Aircraft Co., was a satellite specialist.

Jarvis had twice been bumped from shuttle missions.

Several hundred of Onizuka's relatives reportedly traveled from Hawaii to see the launch.

At 9:30 A.M. Mission Control expressed concern about "one- to two-foot-long" icicles, which could be seen hanging like long beards from the service structure around the spacecraft.

The astronauts were sealed in and the launchpad cleared of ground crew at about 11:10 A.M.

> "NASA officials gathered the news media in the same grandstand from which they had watched the tragedy."

Officials Express Their Sorrow

Four hours after the 11:38 launch, NASA officials gathered the news media in the same grandstand from which they had watched the tragedy and, red-eyed, made an official announcement that the seven crew members had been killed. NASA space flight director Jesse W. Moore, who made the final decision to "go," today expressed his sorrow.

As dusk fell, Vice President [George H.W.] Bush, who last July [1985] announced McAuliffe's selection to fly on the shuttle, arrived at the space center to pay his respects to her family. He was accompanied by Sen. John Glenn (D-Ohio), the first American to orbit the Earth, and Sen. Jake Garn (R-Utah), a veteran of a successful shuttle flight last year who knew the seven aboard.

"We hoped this day would never come," Glenn said. "But unfortunately it has."

Christa McAuliffe's parents had told reporters in recent days that they were "a little scared" for their daughter. But they added that they accepted their daughter's pride and excitement and her strong desire to go.

In the press room, during the days of delay, there had been the usual gallows humor, jokes about having to write stories about how dangerous the flight was—"gang plank" stories about McAuliffe. The attitude was that this was merely hype. After all, no American had been killed in a spacecraft after leaving the launch pad.

McAuliffe had seen herself as a pioneer. It was her study of the 18th century women who crossed America in Conestoga wagons that inspired her to apply for the space trip, she said last July. She had seen the shuttle as her own frontier vehicle.

Explorers such as the astronauts have always been followed by other people, she said. "I look on myself as one of the first of the 'other people.'"

Sharon Christa McAuliffe, a payload specialist, was a teacher and the first private citizen to fly in space, selected from among eleven thousand applicants. She had a year's leave of absence from teaching high school in Concord, New Hampshire, to train for the *Challenger* mission.

The President Speaks to the American People About the Tragedy

Ronald Reagan

On the evening of the *Challenger* disaster, President Ronald Reagan addressed the nation on live television from the Oval Office at the White House. This famous speech, which was written by speechwriter Peggy Noonan, has been ranked as one of the ten best US political speeches of the twentieth century by a group of leading scholars. In it, the president expresses his sorrow and his admiration for the lost astronauts, declaring that the future belongs to the brave, and he promises that space flights including civilians will continue. He concludes with a quotation from the well-known poem "High Flight." Reagan was the fortieth president of the United States and held office from 1981 to 1989.

L adies and gentlemen, I'd planned to speak to you tonight to report on the state of the Union, but the events of earlier today [January 28, 1986] have led me to change those plans. Today is a day for mourn-

SOURCE. Ronald Reagan, Television address, January 28, 1986.

US President Ronald Reagan addresses the nation from the Oval Office on the day of the *Challenger* disaster. The speech became one of his most remembered. (© Diana Walker/Time and Life Pictures/Getty Images.)

ing and remembering. Nancy [the First Lady] and I are pained to the core by the tragedy of the shuttle *Challenger*. We know we share this pain with all of the people of our country. This is truly a national loss.

Nineteen years ago, almost to the day, we lost three astronauts in a terrible accident on the ground. But we've never lost an astronaut in flight; we've never had a tragedy like this. And perhaps we've forgotten the courage it took for the crew of the shuttle. But they, the Challenger Seven, were aware of the dangers, but overcame them and did their jobs brilliantly. We mourn seven heroes: Michael Smith, Dick Scobee, Judith Resnik, Ronald McNair, Ellison Onizuka, Gregory Jarvis, and Christa McAuliffe. We mourn their loss as a nation together.

For the families of the seven, we cannot bear, as you do, the full impact of this tragedy. But we feel the loss,

The Poem "High Flight"

The last sentence of President Ronald Reagan's speech following the *Challenger* disaster contains quotations from the famous poem "High Flight" by John Gillespie Magee Jr. The poem begins with the line, "Oh, I have slipped the surly bonds of earth," and concludes, "With silent, lifting mind I've trod / The high untrespassed sanctity of space, / Put out my hand, and touched the face of God."

Magee was an aviator in World War II and a member of the Royal Canadian Air Force (RCAF) stationed in Britain. He flew in a Spitfire squadron and was killed at the age of nineteen during a routine training mission on December 11, 1941. A few months earlier, he had written the poem on the back of a letter to his parents in which he said that he had started composing it at 30,000 feet and finished soon after he landed. His father, a clergyman, printed it in church publications, where it was seen by the Librarian of Congress and put on display at the library with other poems of "faith and freedom." The original manuscript remains in the Library of Congress collection.

The poem has been reprinted and displayed many times. The RCAF distributed plaques with the words to all its airfields, and it must be recited from memory by freshmen at the US Air Force Academy. It has appeared in middle-school textbooks, has been quoted in books and movies, and has been used by television stations to end their programming day. There have also been musical settings, of which the most familiar is an adaptation by singer/songwriter John Denver.

The entire poem is inscribed on the back of the monument for the *Challenger* astronauts at Arlington National Cemetery.

and we're thinking about you so very much. Your loved ones were daring and brave, and they had that special grace, that special spirit that says, "Give me a challenge, and I'll meet it with joy." They had a hunger to explore the universe and discover its truths. They wished to serve, and they did. They served all of us. We've grown used to wonders in this century. It's hard to dazzle us. But for 25 years the United States space program has been doing just that. We've grown used to the idea of space, and perhaps we forget that we've only just begun. We're still pioneers. They, the members of the *Challenger* crew, were pioneers.

And I want to say something to the schoolchildren of America who were watching the live coverage of the shuttle's takeoff. I know it is hard to understand, but sometimes painful things like this happen. It's all part of the process of exploration and discovery. It's all part of taking a chance and expanding man's horizons. The future doesn't belong to the fainthearted; it belongs to the brave. The *Challenger* crew was pulling us into the future, and we'll continue to follow them.

> The future doesn't belong to the fainthearted; it belongs to the brave.

Space Flight Will Continue

I've always had great faith in and respect for our space program, and what happened today does nothing to diminish it. We don't hide our space program. We don't keep secrets and cover things up. We do it all up front and in public.[1] That's the way freedom is, and we wouldn't change it for a minute. We'll continue our quest in space. There will be more shuttle flights and more shuttle crews and, yes, more volunteers, more civilians, more teachers in space. Nothing ends here; our hopes and our journeys continue. I want to add that I wish I could talk to every man and woman who works for NASA or who worked on this mission and tell them: "Your dedication and professionalism have moved and impressed us for decades. And we know of your anguish. We share it."

There's a coincidence today. On this day 390 years ago, the great explorer Sir Francis Drake died aboard ship off the coast of Panama. In his lifetime the great frontiers were the oceans, and an historian later said, "He lived by the sea, died on it, and was buried in it." Well, today we can say of the *Challenger* crew: Their dedication was, like Drake's, complete.

The crew of the space shuttle *Challenger* honored us by the manner in which they lived their lives. We will never forget them, nor the last time we saw them, this morning, as they prepared for their journey and waved goodbye and "slipped the surly bonds of earth" to "touch the face of God."

Note

1. President Reagan is making a reference to the Soviet Union's policy of keeping its space failures secret.

Crash Creates Worldwide Wave of Shock

Houston Chronicle

In the following viewpoint, a newspaper reports on the worldwide response to the *Challenger* disaster. All over the world, people mourned the loss of *Challenger*, the newspaper states, and many foreign leaders sent messages of condolence to President Ronald Reagan. Even in the Soviet Union—which had been strongly critical of the US shuttle program—the news was more widely reported than was usually the case with US events, and people were shocked and grieved. Sympathy was expressed by the pope, the European Space Agency, and the UN Security Council, among others. West German, Dutch, and French astronauts who had flown on previous shuttle missions also spoke of their sorrow. The Dutch scientist said that those involved in space travel, including the crew of *Challenger*, had all known that there is no such thing as infallibility.

SOURCE. "Crash Creates Worldwide Wave of Shock," *Houston Chronicle*, January 29, 1986. Copyright © 1986 by Houston Chronicle. All rights reserved. Reproduced by permission.

The explosion of the space shuttle *Challenger* plunged much of the world into mourning today for the mission's seven-member crew. Many foreign leaders reacted quickly to the tragedy, sending messages of condolence and support to Washington and in some cases pausing for a moment of mourning.

Soviet leader Mikhail S. Gorbachev told President Reagan today that "we partake of your grief at the tragic death of the crew of the space shuttle *Challenger.*"

However, Poland's state television used the occasion to denounce Reagan's space-based missile defense research venture, calling the explosion a warning of catastrophe that might occur if the United States goes ahead with the program. And the Soviet representative to the United Nations, Vasiliy S. Safronchuk, dropped hints along the same lines.

The Soviets have often criticized the U.S. shuttle program, charging that it is helping an American program to militarize space.

In the Soviet Union, however, the state-run media reported the disaster without propagandizing.

Just two hours after the shuttle exploded, Tuesday's evening news show broadcast film of the tragedy to about 180 million Soviet viewers. Today, five of the country's leading newspapers, including the Communist Party newspaper *Pravda*, carried full reports on the disaster.

Muscovites who had seen the television film or heard the news expressed shock when interviewed. They particularly were upset that two women had been killed.

The swiftness and detail of the reporting contrasted with the secrecy that normally surrounds the Soviet space program, especially its failures.

In Rome, Pope John Paul II today described the astronauts as "courageous pioneers" for human progress. Addressing nearly 5,000 pilgrims gathered for his weekly general audience, the pope said the tragedy caused "deep pain" for people around the world. The Vatican said the

A man in Beijing holds a copy of *China Daily*, China's English-language newspaper on January 30, 1986. (© **Neal Ulevich/Associated Press.**)

pontiff also sent a telegram to Reagan, expressing his condolences.

Brazilian President Jose Sarney, a poet, sent a message to Reagan expressing his "most profound solidarity and condolences."

"The United States, throughout its history, has managed to face great challenges in moments of anguish, but the strength of its people and of its great destiny have always been greater than the tragedy," Sarney said. "This strength represents the most comforting prayer at this time.

"The efforts the United States has carried out to conquer space," he said, "are a permanent lesson in the capacity of man to out-do himself, to turn some of his greatest dreams into reality."

President Miguel de la Madrid of Mexico extended his deepest condolences both to the families of the crew and to the officials of the space agency. "It was with great sorrow that I learned of the tragic accident suffered by the space shuttle *Challenger*," he wrote Reagan Tuesday afternoon. "I deeply regret this tragedy."

Rodolfo Neri Vela, the Mexican astronaut who flew on the shuttle *Atlantis* in November, said he could not believe the news at first: "I could not accept the idea that this could happen. This is a national tragedy for the United States but I believe it is a tragedy for the world as well."

Prime Minister Brian Mulroney of Canada sent a message of condolence to Reagan. But the prime minister added that the accident "ought not discourage us from participating in this great adventure."

The Canadian House of Commons observed a moment of silence in memory of *Challenger*'s crew. And the Canadian consul in Dallas, Douglas H.M. Branion, said, "We share a great loss and sympathize with the families. Canada is a neighbor and a close ally in the U.S. space effort." A Canadian astronaut, Marc Garneau, flew in *Challenger* in 1984.

The Cuban government issued a statement expressing its "condolences to the American people for this painful tragedy." An announcer on Cuba's nightly television newscast said after running the videotape of the disaster: "The people of Cuba cannot repress their sensitivity to this tragedy."

Ernst Messerschmidt, one of two West German astronauts who flew in *Challenger* in November, said: "It is terrible to see these pictures, especially when you know some of the people involved. It's even harder to think that it could have been you."

Wubbo Ockels, a Dutch scientist who also flew on *Challenger* in November, said he was "terribly shocked and terribly sad" about the disaster. "NASA has done everything to guarantee safety," he said, "but there's no such thing as infallibility, and the seven knew that and so did we all."

President Francois Mitterrand of France said: "It has always been the destiny of courageous people, discoverers of new worlds, to pay such a heavy tribute to progress."

The U.N. Security Council paused at the start of debate in New York to extend condolences to the United States.

> 'It has always been the destiny of courageous people, discoverers of new worlds, to pay such a heavy tribute to progress.'

"Deep sympathy with NASA" came from the European Space Agency. The accident was "a disaster for NASA and for space in general, and as ESA is in space, a disaster for us," spokesman Jean-Paul Paille said in Paris.

Paille's agency builds the Ariane satellite launcher as a commercial rival to the shuttle, but cooperates closely with NASA on other projects and built the Spacelab carried on previous shuttle flights.

French astronaut Patrick Baudry, who also took part in a shuttle flight, praised NASA's training program and the shuttle.

"Once you get inside, you have great confidence in the machine, the team. NASA takes no risks." He added, however, that space technology was so complex and delicate that "there is no routine yet."

Prime Minister Margaret Thatcher of Britain, Prime Minister Rajiv Gandhi of India, King Hussein of Jordan and Prime Minister Garret Fitzgerald of Ireland sent messages to Reagan expressing condolences.

In other reaction, President Pieter Botha of South Africa said: "All South Africans were stunned by the tragic news of the explosion. The free world has followed the United States space program with pride."

Students at Christa McAuliffe's High School Are Stunned by Grief

Michael Shanahan

In the following viewpoint, a journalist details how the students of Concord High School in New Hampshire, where Christa McAuliffe taught, were celebrating and cheering as they watched the *Challenger* launch on television. They stopped blowing noise-makers when they began to realize, with shock, that she was gone. Classes were cancelled for the rest of that day and the next one. McAuliffe had been a popular and inspiring teacher who had given her students an understanding of the people who made history. She had told them she wanted them to reach for the stars. The whole town had been excited when she was chosen to go into space and had given her a parade; another had been planned for her return. It was too soon, officials said, to find a way to honor her memory. Michael Shanahan was a staff writer for the *Sacramento Bee*, a Sacramento, California, newspaper.

SOURCE. Michael Shanahan, "Joyful Cries Died on Lips," *Sacramento Bee*, January 29, 1986. Copyright © 1986 by Sacramento Bee. All rights reserved. Reproduced by permission.

One by one, the students of Concord High School stopped blowing dozens of party noisemakers celebrating the launching of their favorite teacher into space as the first citizen astronaut.

Gathered before televisions in the high school auditorium, the students had counted down, "Five, four, three, two, one," as the space shuttle *Challenger* began its voyage with Christa McAuliffe, popular social-studies teacher and mother of two, on board.

They cheered as the shuttle slowly lifted from the launch pad after three days of frustrating delays.

But shouts of joy were gradually replaced by stunned, cold silence as the realization sank in that McAuliffe had died in a ball of flame inside the shuttle.

"This couldn't happen," said Kristin Tousignant, a junior at the school. "Everybody was just staring and staring and staring. There was just quiet silence for so long."

"It was just weird," said Jeff Savoy, 16. "Everyone was so happy she was going into space."

"We thought, 'Well, finally she made it off,' and then they said, 'Major malfunction,'" said Savoy, also a junior. "After we went back to the classroom, the teachers were as stunned as we were."

"Our bubble has burst," said another student.

> McAuliffe had the rare genius given to a few teachers able to inspire even the most reluctant student to learn.

By all accounts, McAuliffe had the rare genius given to a few teachers able to inspire even the most reluctant student to learn. Her own enthusiasm for life was infectious inside the classroom.

"She told her kids she wanted them to reach for the stars," her principal, Charles Foley, said a few hours after the space shuttle exploded. "That was her legacy."

"She loved teaching, she loved her students," he said. "She was an exciting person."

A student stands by an impromptu memorial outside Concord High School in New Hampshire, where Christa McAuliffe was a teacher, a few days after the *Challenger* disaster. (© **Elise Amendola/AP Images.**)

"She had a great sense of living and joy," Foley said. "We have all learned that life is full of uncertainty and even the best plans can go awry. We are going to have to teach our kids to deal with the fact that nothing is predictable."

McAuliffe Was a Local Celebrity

Concord is the kind of town where they give parades when one of their own achieves national recognition. Indeed, there was precedent. One of the original astronauts, Alan Shepard, of nearby Derry, had become a national hero.

And so it was last July [1985] when McAuliffe was selected the winner from more than 11,000 applicants who accepted President Reagan's invitation to apply to become the first teacher in space.

The 37-year-old McAuliffe was given a police escort into town when she returned from Washington where the selection was announced on the White House lawn.

"WOW" headlined the *Concord Monitor*, the local daily newspaper.

About 2,500 persons from among the city's population of 32,000 lined Main Street to watch the slender McAuliffe, wearing a light blue NASA jump suit, ride by in a convertible.

At her side were her children, Scott, 9, and Caroline, 6.

Her husband Steven, a local lawyer, took pictures of his wife from a truck in the parade as it wound through this small state capital nestled in the foothills of the White Mountains in central New Hampshire.

> 'It's had a bigger shock than the day the president was shot because of the local impact.'

Along Main Street on Tuesday [January 28, 1986], a chill wind and near zero temperatures only added to the grief and sorrow.

Most said they wanted to bear their loss quietly.

But Jim Makris, manager of the Talk of the Town restaurant on Main Street said, "It's had a bigger shock than the day the president [Ronald Reagan] was shot because of the local impact and because there was such a big buildup. People have been somber," he said.

About 40 lunchtime customers had gathered to watch the liftoff in the restaurant, and instead looked

The Challenger Center

After the *Challenger* disaster, the families of the seven astronauts who perished wanted to create a permanent memorial. June Scobee Rodgers, the widow of shuttle commander Dick Scobee, wrote, "We just couldn't let the words 'Challenger' or 'space' mean something sad for children. So the idea of a living tribute to carry on the educational mission of the crew developed into Challenger Center. This tribute would utilize the excitement of space to inspire and motivate our nation's schoolchildren to take interest in mathematics, science, and technology."

Led by the families, a campaign was launched to raise $1 million in startup funds for an educational center, and in 1988, Congress established a $15 million trust fund. That year, the first Challenger Learning Center opened at the Houston Museum of Natural Science. Today there are more than fifty Challenger Learning Centers located in thirty-one states and

on in horror as bits of the *Challenger* fell into the Atlantic Ocean more than 1,000 miles to the south. "We had customers crying," said Makris. "It just devastated everybody."

Officials canceled classes for Tuesday and today [January 29, 1986] inside the brick, high-columned high school where McAuliffe taught, although teachers, guidance counselors and psychologists were available for anyone who wanted to talk over the loss.

A Period of Official Mourning

The state Legislature also recessed. And Gov. John H. Sununu declared a period of official mourning in a state which usually gains national prominence only every four years because of its early presidential primary election.

Memorial services were held at Framingham State College in Massachusetts where McAuliffe earned her several other countries, with more opening every year. More than five hundred thousand students participate in their programs, which include simulated space missions, and more than six thousand teachers learn to use Challenger Center materials in their classrooms.

In a "Letter to America" on the first anniversary of the disaster, the families wrote that the astronauts were "people who worked hard to extend the reach of the human race no matter what the sac- rifice. They risked their lives, not for the sake of aimless adventure, but for the nation that gave them opportunity, and for the space frontier which was an extension of its spirit. . . . The Challenger Center is our idea of a fitting tribute, a celebration of our loved ones' lives, a triumph over their loss. We hope that by making space-like experiences accessible to all people, especially children, we can prepare them for the day when they will take their own place among the stars."

undergraduate degree, and at St. Jeremiah's Roman Catholic Church in the same Boston suburb where her parents, Edward and Grace Corrigan, are still parishioners.

The Corrigans were poor when Christa was an infant and the family lived in a one-bedroom apartment near Boston's Fenway Park while her father finished college.

In Concord, which had planned a huge welcome home celebration and rally in March for McAuliffe, officials said it was too early to find a way to honor her memory.

When she applied to become a citizen astronaut, McAuliffe said she wanted to keep a journal so she could "humanize" the experience. "I want to demystify NASA and space flight," she said then. "I want students to see and understand the special perspective of space and relate it to them."

One of McAuliffe's former students, Mike Dillon, said once in an interview that she was a special teacher because she translated the changing tides of history into an understanding of the people who made history. "She gives the lesson and then she has a little story to tell," Dillon said.

> [McAuliffe] was a special teacher because she translated the changing tides of history into an understanding of the people who made history.

Concord residents and others who knew McAuliffe said she knew there was the possibility that something could go wrong on the 25th shuttle flight.

"I think we all knew there was danger," said teacher Charles Sposato, also of Framingham, Mass., and coincidentally a semifinalist in the competition to become an astronaut.

"We were told of the risks," he said.

US Psyche Rattled: Shuttle Blast Exposed Human, Technological Fragility

E.A. Torriero and Dan Nakaso

In the following viewpoint, two journalists speculate about why the *Challenger* accident affected the American public so much more deeply than other disasters that took more lives. Maybe, they say, it was because people saw it replayed many times on television. Maybe it was because a schoolteacher was aboard, or because the crew included a representative variety of Americans of different races and religions, showing that ordinary people—not just superheroes—could go into space. Or maybe it was because everyone had believed that the nation's space program would remain as successful as it had been in the past, unblemished by serious setbacks. Finally, the authors suggest that the tragedy made people aware of their own mortality. E.A. Torriero and Dan Nakaso were staff writers for the *San Jose Mercury News*.

SOURCE. E.A. Torriero and Dan Nakaso, "U.S. Psyche Rattled: Shuttle Blast Exposed Human, Technological Fragility," *San Jose Mercury News*, February 2, 1986. Copyright © 1986 by San Jose Mercury News. All rights reserved. Reproduced by permission.

Why did it shake our national consciousness? Why did news of Tuesday's [January 28, 1986] shuttle explosion leave shoppers in a Boston supermarket in tears; halt congressional business in Washington, D.C.; move the people of Atchison, Kan., to send batches of flowers; prompt teachers in some Midwest cities to wear black armbands; cause Los Angeles officials to relight the Olympic torch for a day; and lead a San Jose mother of two to hold an impromptu candlelight vigil?

"It's been a long time since this country has been this shook up," said Donna Slack, an electronics technician who works with the shuttle simulator at the Johnson Space Center here [Houston, Texas].

"People will remember this like they do the Kennedy assassination," Slack said Friday as she waited for President [Ronald] Reagan to speak at the ceremony honoring the seven astronauts who lost their lives in the mission.

> Nothing in recent memory has so rattled the American psyche . . . as the shuttle tragedy.

"People will always remember where they were when they heard about the explosion," she said. "It's hit people that hard."

America has suffered through so many tragedies in recent years, tragedies that have taken many more lives—airliner crashes, terrorist hijackings and bombings.

But nothing in recent memory has so rattled the American psyche—and left the country so full of remorse—as the shuttle tragedy.

Maybe it was caused by the horror of seeing the explosion replayed on television.

Maybe it was the crew members, who seemed to represent nearly every side of America.

Maybe it was the loss of Christa McAuliffe, a teacher, a mother and the first private citizen in space, who assured us that shuttle travel probably was "safer than driving on the streets of New York."

Maybe it was the loss of the national conviction that nothing could mar the nation's cherished space program.

Maybe it was the way the shuttle abruptly disappeared in a plume of smoke.

"The shuttle explosion left a psychological wake that ripples from those closest to the astronauts and NASA out to the entire American people," Mardi Horowitz, a psychiatrist at the University of California at San Francisco told the *New York Times*.

"In that wake is the sense of a world crumbling," said Horowitz, considered an expert in the psychological effects of disasters. "It's a shocking symbol of the fragility of all our hopes, of human technology, and finally of human life."

Within minutes of the crash Tuesday morning, millions of Americans in offices and homes turned on their televisions to hear news of the explosion. Over and over, viewers saw replays and close-ups of the disaster; taped reactions of the crew's shaken relatives who had been watching the launch; and film of teen-agers in Concord, N.H., who saw their teacher's spacecraft blow up.

In one sequence, the cameras caught the reaction of Ed and Grace Corrigan, Christa McAuliffe's parents, as their elation at the liftoff turned into shock. The images were psychologically paralyzing.

"It's one thing to bring a tragedy to your attention, once it's happened," said George Gerbner, a University of Pennsylvania communications professor. "It's another to witness it with the feeling that you're witnessing history." Added Philip Zimbardo, a Stanford University psychology professor: "We not only saw the shuttle explode and kill the astronauts, we also saw the reaction of the parents of one of them. . . . We have the grief of the mother and the disbelief of the father, and we see it before our eyes. That affected us greatly."

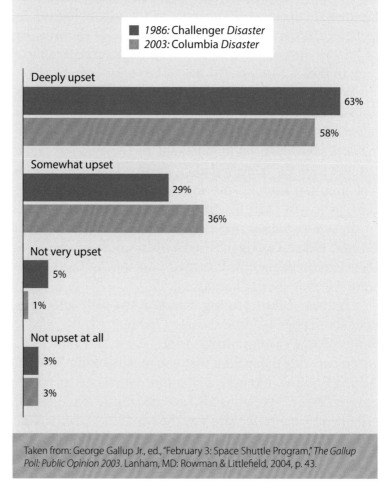

THE US PUBLIC WAS GREATLY DISTRESSED BY THE *CHALLENGER* AND *COLUMBIA* DISASTERS

Between January 31 and February 3, 1986, a Louis Harris and Associates poll asked members of the public: "When the space shuttle *Challenger* blew up this past week, did you personally feel deeply upset, somewhat upset, not very upset, or not upset at all?" Nearly two decades later, on February 2, 2003, a Gallup poll asked members of the public: "When the space shuttle *Columbia* was lost yesterday, did you personally feel deeply upset, somewhat upset, not very upset, or not upset at all?" In both occasions nearly two-thirds of the public said they were deeply upset by the space shuttle tragedies.

■ *1986:* Challenger *Disaster*
■ *2003:* Columbia *Disaster*

Deeply upset
63%
58%

Somewhat upset
29%
36%

Not very upset
5%
1%

Not upset at all
3%
3%

Taken from: George Gallup Jr., ed., "February 3: Space Shuttle Program," *The Gallup Poll: Public Opinion 2003*. Lanham, MD: Rowman & Littlefield, 2004, p. 43.

Even before the crash, there was a heightened interest in what was the 25th shuttle mission. It was Spaceship America—on board were a black, a Japanese American, a Jew, Protestants, two women and five men.

In their spare time, the crew members operated karate schools, served as church deacons, played jazz and raised middle-class American families.

> It was Spaceship America—on board were a black, a Japanese American, a Jew, Protestants, two women and five men.

"This particular flight had a unique, symbolic meaning" because of McAuliffe, said Tom Wolfe, author of *The Right Stuff,* in an interview with *U.S. News & World Report.* "It really was designed to mean the end, once and for all, of the era of the 'right stuff.'

"No longer did you think of people who go into space as dauntless pioneers and very special people with nerves of steel."

Unlike some of the shuttle missions, which were kept secret, Mission 51-L was a widely advertised space adventure. It was to have included several live school lessons for America's students.

"Many people followed every step of this preparation for the shuttle and felt as if it were happening to them," said Wendy Martyna, who teaches courses in death and dying at the University of California at Santa Cruz. "In a sense, each of us was up there with them and we identified with that.

"It could have been one of us."

At the center of that identity was McAuliffe, the 37-year-old social studies teacher who was selected as the finalist in the teacher-in-space program from among 11,146 applicants. Bubbly, full of civic pride and wide-eyed at the opportunity to voyage into space, McAuliffe—a mother of two with a husband who is a lawyer—seemed to be part of a textbook all-American family.

She hoped she could bridge the gap between the complexities of science and ordinary people. "My perceptions as a non-astronaut would help complete and humanize the technology of the Space Age," she wrote in an essay for the National Aeronautics and Space Administration [NASA] competition. "Future historians would use my eyewitness accounts to help in their studies of the impact of the Space Age on the general population."

In that essay, McAuliffe wrote that she proudly recalled "a cloudy, rainy night driving through Pennsylvania and hearing the news that the astronauts had landed safely."

The first teacher-naut was so imbued with the certainty of space travel that last July [1985] she told an interviewer, "Today's shuttle isn't the type of thing, I think, that anybody really looks at with fear that there's going to be some accident. I feel probably safer doing something like that than driving around the New York streets."

And Americans were so convinced she was right that hundreds of thousands of school children were allowed to watch the launch in classrooms, auditoriums and at the Kennedy Space Center.

Since the explosion—while psychologists worry about the effects the disaster will have on children—McAuliffe has become an almost mythic hero. "She was much larger in death perhaps than in life," said Charles Foley, the principal of the high school where McAuliffe taught social studies. "What happened is incomprehensible."

It happened just as space missions had begun to seem routine.

In the last two decades, since one of America's first unmanned rockets failed on the launch pad, more than 50 space missions have had glorious endings. With the exception of a fire that killed three astronauts on the launch pad in 1967, there have been few mishaps.

And never before Tuesday had an American died in space.

The nation's astronauts have been crossing frontier after frontier, notching "attaboys" for the American history scrapbook and fueling the country's seemingly endless fascination with space.

"What is it that makes a man willing to sit on top of an enormous Roman Candle . . . and wait for someone to light the fuse?" Wolfe asked in *The Right Stuff*.

At least one astronaut had an answer for Wolfe.

"Exploration without man is not exploration at all," said Eugene A. Cernan, the last astronaut to walk on the moon.

Author James Michener recalled *Challenger* astronaut Judith Resnik's impatience with all the delays of the space program.

Fifth and sixth graders in a Hollywood, California, school make crafts in February 1986 to express their sympathy for the *Challenger* crew. Many observers believe that the disaster led to a loss of innocence for children of the era. (© **Ben Martin/Time and Life Pictures/Getty Images.**)

"Get me into space before I'm an old woman," Michener remembers her imploring. "They are moving so slow. I want to get out there."

Like fast cars, space travel became a part of the American scene. Some enterprising travel agencies were offering possible bookings on shuttle rides of the future and eventual trips to the moon. Already there is a waiting list.

And when *Challenger* suddenly blew apart on a crisp Florida morning, a symbol of national pride deflated.

"The shuttle has played a powerful role in our collective fantasy life as a symbol of an American dream," said Horowitz, the San Francisco psychiatrist. "It's an image etched into our minds of American power."

American space agency power was used this week to comb the Atlantic Ocean for debris and to analyze computer data from the shuttle in hopes of pinning a cause to the explosion. Despite millions of dollars spent on the technology to avert such disasters—and the knowledge gained from problems encountered on other space missions—NASA officials for the time being are baffled.

"There was nothing anyone could have done for this one," launch flight director Jay Green said Wednesday. "It just stopped."

For many Americans, that explanation was unsettling and appeared only to fuel a growing sense of national guilt. Some NASA engineers muttered last week about their feelings of failure. In their remorse, some Americans wondered if the nation had become too blasé about space travel.

"I think maybe people have gotten overconfident—they think they are dealing with a commercial airline or a Disney ride," Mercury astronaut Donald "Deke" Slayton said Wednesday.

As President Reagan vowed last week that the shuttle program will continue, those who helped put *Challenger* in the air—and who watched helplessly as it fell—are waiting for some answers.

"We need to find a cause," said Wayne Green, a space engineer who has worked on the components of Mission Control at the space center. "Once we know what has happened, we can move on.

"Just seeing that shuttle blow up, and not knowing why, is difficult to deal with."

> The shuttle's legacy may be that it gave Americans an uneasy sense of their own mortality.

As the grieving continues, a new generation of Americans will not soon forget the image of an exploding *Challenger*, a grim lesson that science and America are not infallible.

"I always wanted to be an astronaut," one young child said in a national newscast this week. "But I've changed my mind. I don't want to die."

The shuttle's legacy may be that it gave Americans an uneasy sense of their own mortality.

"People spend a lot of time ignoring that death is going to happen to them," said Lynne DeSpelder, who teaches at the University of California at Santa Cruz and has authored a book on death and dying. "People put death in a closet. And this blew the hinges off the closet."

CHAPTER 2

Controversies Concerning the *Challenger* Disaster

Are Manned Flights Needed?

Mary McGrory

In the following viewpoint, a journalist argues that Christa McAuliffe should not have been aboard the *Challenger*. McAuliffe had two young children who wanted her to stay home, and the author believes that being a mother and teacher is more important than pioneering. In her opinion, space flights should be left to the professional astronauts and even then, the risks of manned space flight are unjustified. Such flights serve only to popularize the space program, she says, and are unnecessary because unmanned spacecraft can bring back information for science. Mary McGrory was a journalist and political columnist who won the Pulitzer Prize for her coverage of the Watergate scandal.

Photo on previous page: Workers hoist wreckage of the *Challenger* pulled from the Atlantic Ocean onto a loading platform at Cape Canaveral, Florida, in January 1986. (© **Space Frontiers/Archive Photos/Getty Images.**)

T he catastrophe at Cape Canaveral has rocked the country in a special way.

Upon being advised that the *Challenger* had blown up, the president asked, "Is that the one the

SOURCE. Mary McGrory, "Are Manned Flights Needed?," *Dallas Morning News*, January 31, 1986. Copyright © 1986 by Dallas Morning News. All rights reserved. Reproduced by permission.

teacher was on?"—unerringly putting his finger on the source of the explosion of public and official dismay.

The 10th flight of the space shuttle *Challenger* was to most Americans, other than the families and friends of the six other brave people on board, the flight of Christa McAuliffe, a high school teacher from Concord, N.H.

Bound for glory, she was killed 74 seconds after takeoff, almost 10 miles up. She never made it to outer space. A mysterious explosion tore the *Challenger* apart, distorted its silver bullet shape into a surrealistic outline of a gigantic exotic bird with a grotesquely long neck.

As millions watched open-mouthed, a parachute appeared on the screen. It was a flash of false hopes. It belonged to rescue workers who could find nothing to rescue.

The faces of Mrs. McAuliffe's parents were shown, jubilant at first, then frozen in horror.

The question is: Why was she there? She wanted to be, no question. She had eagerly participated in the National Aeronautics and Space Administration's most ambitious public relations campaign, a contest to choose the first teacher to be blasted off the earth.

She knew, she said, in one of the innumerable interviews she cheerfully gave after her selection from among 11,000 applicants, that NASA would benefit enormously from her presence on the craft, but it didn't bother her. She thought the rewards for a teacher would be comparable. Two rather hokey capsule-classroom sessions were planned—an exercise NASA thought would give earthlings a new enthusiasm for its expensive and increasingly frequent shuttle launches.

Mrs. McAuliffe had the right stuff. She was an exceptionally winning and buoyant personality. She seemed the kind of person who could cope with the multiple demands made on space-age women. She was a wife, a teacher and a mother. The training program that took her away from home, the coming claims of greater celebrity, all seemed within her management.

She had two children, Scott, age 9, and Caroline, age 6. Over and over again, after the television replays of the horror, we heard that Caroline had not wanted her mother to go into space. We watched her saying she wanted her mother in the house.

The catastrophe at Canaveral will occasion questions about sending civilians on dangerous missions, especially mothers of young children. What Mrs. McAuliffe taught us—posthumously, to our grief—is that there are limits to technology. It made us wonder if a space capsule is the place for amateurs. The others were professional astronauts, trained for danger. Mrs. McAuliffe put her total faith in official declarations that space travel is quite safe.

Almost immediately, a chorus formed to say that the only proper memorial to Mrs. McAuliffe and the six teammates who died with her was to continue the space program. It was led by the president, who said, "There will be more shuttle flights and more shuttle crews and, yes, more volunteers, more civilians, more teachers in space."

Christa McAuliffe accepts her nomination to be the first teacher chosen for the NASA program from US vice president George H.W. Bush. Some cite her death as a prime example of why manned space travel is too dangerous. (© Cynthia Johnson/Time and Life Pictures/Getty Images.)

But should there be? Professor Thomas Gold, a respected astronomer at Cornell University, appeared on the *MacNeil/Lehrer NewsHour* while the networks were pouring out reminiscences, data and conjecture about the cause of the blow-up to say that manned flights are unnecessary and wrong. Unmanned space flights bring back as much information without gigantic risks to astronauts—"Look what we are getting from Uranus with instruments," Gold said.

"Sending up human beings is merely for public relations, to popularize the space program. It is easy to say it afterward, but I said it before this disaster," the professor said in a telephone interview. "These people are not performing serious scientific experiments. They are passing the time in space and make the pretense that the public is involved. It was a terrible thing for NASA even to suggest it. The idea of sending people on this dicey business for public display while we are short-changing the utilitarian and scientific programs is ludicrous."

The implications of the *Challenger* tragedy are unsettling, and not just for the space program. The president must consider that Star Wars, a space-based program, is the ultimate in the high technology that failed the *Challenger*. Its premise is that millions of gadgets, with hairline timing, will function flawlessly on computer demand when missiles start flying.

That proposition is now in deeper doubt, especially among people who think that Earth's solutions will be provided on Earth—and that we cannot spare good teachers.

> 'Sending up human beings [into space] is merely for public relations, to popularize the space program.'

Despite Risks, Manned Space Flight Must Continue

Richmond Times-Dispatch

In the following viewpoint, published a day after the *Challenger* disaster, a newspaper editorial argues that space exploration is an indispensable dream of humankind. Humans are, and will continue to be, needed to man space flights, the newspaper maintains, and it is inevitable that some will pay with their lives. This was the fifty-sixth manned US space mission and the tenth for *Challenger*. Despite problems, all the previous ones were successful, the newspaper asserts, so people had begun to take space flight for granted. Yet death is a risk for all spacefarers who confront the future courageously, says the writer. The risks they take is what makes them heroes, and none of those on board *Challenger* would have said that manned space flight should stop. Hope and risk have been ingredients of every step forward ever taken by humankind, the author asserts, and the astronauts' hope of reaching the stars must not go unfulfilled.

SOURCE. "Challenger, RIP," *Richmond Times-Dispatch*, January 29, 1986. Copyright © 1986 by Richmond Times-Dispatch. All rights reserved. Reproduced by permission.

This isn't supposed to happen to dreams—especially not to this dream. In perhaps mankind's most ambitious adventure, through our astronauts we are living the dream of eons. They and the specialists who ride with them are agents of the redeeming myth we need so much. Until we build space machines that render human beings obsolete, we shall require human beings to man them. And some, as happened grimly yesterday, will pay their full measure atop a pillar of fire.

Sitting in the stands at lift-off, as we have done, one waits through the lighting of the launch-pad fuse for the staggering horror that—until yesterday [January 28, 1986]—never came to the American space program. This was the 56th manned space flight in the program's 25 years—the 25th shuttle flight, the 10th for *Challenger*. When you're working at the knife-edge of such revolutionary technology, there is—there can be—no fail-safes. Many of those flights were dogged by technical foulups and human mistakes. But all ended in more or less success; all, until yesterday, brought their human cargo home. For what inevitably happened yesterday, no preparation can be adequate. Yet such a success had America's manned space program become, and so routine its flights, that despite the special hype for this *Challenger* flight because it carried a teacher, none of the major television networks broadcast the lift-off live. We long had taken space flight for granted; we should not anymore.

Death is a risk facing anyone who confronts the future with the audacity of these spacefarers from this—the first spacefaring nation. Are they heroes? They are indeed. For no matter the redundancy built into the rocketry that carries them skyward, and no matter how much they know (and we know) about the scientific systems and the safety features that make space flight possible, their courage lies undiminished. Heroes give men their bearings; they are heroes largely because of the risks they take. Fear deposed by knowledge does not render brav-

Christa McAuliffe Knew the Risk

At the time of the *Challenger* tragedy, the media had been treating space shuttle launches as routine, thus giving the impression that space flight had become a normal, safe activity, and the Teacher in Space program reinforced that idea. As a result, the public was not only grief-stricken but astonished by the disaster. Many people believed that a private citizen should not have been sent into space. Some of them assumed that Christa McAuliffe had been no more aware of the risk than they themselves were, to the dismay of those who believed she was not given due credit for her bravery.

Everyone knowledgeable about space flight knew that it was risky. A person seriously considering being propelled into space by flaming rocket engines producing 6.5 million pounds of thrust would have been aware of the danger. McAuliffe had trained with the professional astronauts for months, and all astronauts realize that space missions place them in harm's way. Moreover, other teachers who applied for the flight stated that they had been warned. McAuliffe said in interviews that she was not worried, but that did not mean she was ignorant.

Richard Feynman, a well-known physicist who was a member of the commission that investigated the accident, wrote: "This has had very unfortunate consequences, the most serious of which is to encourage ordinary citizens to fly in such a dangerous machine, as if it had attained the safety of an ordinary airliner. The astronauts, like test pilots, should know their risks, and we honor them for their courage. Who can doubt that McAuliffe was equally a person of great courage, who was closer to an awareness of the true risk than NASA management would have us believe?"

While not everyone considers the risks of space flight worth taking, Christa McAuliffe thought they were and took them knowingly.

ery redundant. Yesterday's seven were true to Seneca's observation, "Courage leads starward."

Properly, this awful incident should suspend the shuttle program until we can learn whatever can be learned about yesterday's whys. And then, improvements and adjustments made, we should press on. We must. None aboard *Challenger* yesterday would have argued

Christa McAuliffe (second from left) trains with her replacement Barbara Morgan (second from right) and other NASA crew before their ill-fated mission. Some argue that the crew would urge NASA to continue the space program, despite their deaths. Barbara Morgan went on to pursue a career as an astronaut. (© NASA/ Getty Images.)

for a cessation of manned space flight as a result of what happened. On the contrary, all would have argued that despite this setback we should proceed. All, from the place on some spatial shore they now know for the first time, might cite that as *Challenger's* ultimate challenge— its essential lesson.

Hope and risk: They are the fundamental ingredients of every probe and quest ever undertaken by man. They stood with him in Stone Age caves, at Thermopylae, at Calvary; aboard the explorers' ships, on the American frontier, at Kitty Hawk; and they stand with him at Canaveral. Risk gives victory its meaning. For the seven, risk was fulfilled yesterday eight miles down range from Canaveral, 10 miles up. We must not allow their hope to go, as a consequence, unfulfilled. We must not permit our candle to be blown out.

There are, today, somber speculations about the space program. It must not die. We are but flecks of dust on a tiny backwater planet, circling a second-rate star, in a trillion-mile whirlpool we call the solar system. Yet we are poised at the brink of the cosmic wilderness, confronting the untrodden heights, ready to venture away from this third planet from the sun into the interstellar deeps. That is our dream, our extraterrestrial imperative. The manned space program has enabled us to begin the incomparable climb. None of the seven who died fiery deaths before our eyes yesterday would suggest, ever, that we not go on.

> None of the seven who died fiery deaths before our eyes yesterday would suggest, ever, that we not go on.

No Misconduct Was Involved in the Decision to Launch *Challenger*

Diane Vaughan, interviewed by Bertrand Villeret

In the following viewpoint, a sociologist explains that when she began investigating the Challenger accident, she assumed that NASA managers had broken safety rules in order to meet the launch schedule. She later learned that this was not the case. In any large organization, she says, people go on doing what they have done successfully in the past because they come to consider it as normal. For example, although NASA had noticed problems with the O-rings after previous shuttle flights, these problems had not caused any failures before, so managers felt that they were not dangerous. In her opinion, this is why early warning signs of trouble are often ignored. Diane Vaughan is a professor of sociology at Columbia University. She is noted for her book *The Challenger Launch Decision* and was a member of the board that investigated the later accident of the space shuttle Columbia. Bertrand Villeret is editor-in-chief of the French website *Consulting Newsline*.

SOURCE. Diane Vaughan, interviewed by Bertrand Villeret, "Interview: Diane Vaughan," *Consulting Newsline*, May 2008. Copyright © 2008 by Diane Vaughan. All rights reserved. Reproduced by permission.

*B*ertrand Villeret: So we get to the core of your research work and your main contribution to the
field: Deviance and acceptance of deviance. Might
you develop this concept for our readers, most involved in
management consulting?

Diane Vaughan: The *Challenger* case is a good example.
Initially, it appeared to be a case of individuals—NASA
managers—under competitive pressure who violated
rules about launching the shuttle in order to meet the
launch schedule. It was the violation of the rules in pursuit
of organization goals that made it seem like misconduct
to me. But after getting deeper into the data, it turned out
the managers had not violated rules at all, but had actually conformed to all NASA requirements. After analysis
I realized that people conformed to "other rules" than the
regular procedures. They were conforming to the agency's
need to meet schedules, engineering rules about how to
make decisions about risk. These rules were about what
were acceptable risks for the technologies of space flight.
We discovered that they could set up the rules that conformed to the basic engineering principles that allowed
them to accept more and more risk. So they established a
social normalization of the deviance, meaning once they
accepted the first technical anomaly, they continued to
accept more and more with each launch. It was not deviant to them. In their view, they were conforming to engineering and organizational principles. That was the big
[discovery]. I concluded it was mistake, not misconduct.

A discovery . . . a Challenger, *plus a* Columbia. *. . . May
we compare the observed behaviours to the one of drivers
running on empty, for instance . . . "so far so good"?*

Yes, you succeed by risking a little, you don't fail, so each
time you risk a little more. What is different from your
driving example is the role of the organization in urging
you along in this risky business.

The *Columbia* Disaster

On February 1, 2003—almost exactly seventeen years after the *Challenger* disaster—another space shuttle disintegrated, killing its entire crew. This time it was *Columbia*, which broke apart on reentry into the atmosphere after completion of its mission. The cause was an accident which, unknown to anyone, had occurred during launch: a small piece of foam had broken off the shuttle's main fuel tank and debris had hit the leading edge of the orbiter's left wing. This damaged the tiles of the thermal protection system, resulting in the wing's destruction when it was subjected to the heat of reentry.

Some engineers suspected that there was damage while *Columbia* was still in orbit, but at that point there was nothing either they or the crew could have done about it, so no investigation of the possibility was completed. The underlying problem was the same as with *Challenger*—NASA managers had become so used to minor foam shedding that they did not consider it dangerous. Afterward, the shuttle program was suspended for several years while NASA's operations were reassessed.

Construction of the International Space Station (ISS) was put on hold, but it was decided that in addition to other new safety measures, future shuttle missions would be flown only to the ISS so that the crew could stay in it while waiting for rescue if that should be needed.

Columbia's crew of five men and two women included Rick Husband, commander; William McCool, pilot; David Brown, Kalpana Chawla, and Laurel Clark, mission specialists; Michael Anderson, payload commander; and Israeli Air Force Colonel Ilan Ramon, payload specialist.

The United States and the world mourned the loss of *Columbia*'s crew, but there was less shock and surprise than there had been at the loss of *Challenger*, because many people had expected that someday there would be another disaster. Nevertheless, the incident further weakened enthusiasm for the manned space program—although the majority of Americans still supported it—and contributed to the decision to retire the remaining three shuttles by 2010 (later extended to 2011).

Deviance, normalization of deviance. What was exactly that normalization of deviance in the case of NASA?

Social normalization of deviance means that people within the organization become so much accustomed to a deviant behaviour that they don't consider it as deviant, despite the fact that they far exceed their own rules for the elementary safety. But it is a complex process with some kind of organizational acceptance. The people outside see the situation as deviant whereas the people inside get accustomed to it and do not. The more they do it, the more they get accustomed.

For instance in the *Challenger* case there were design flaws in the famous "O-rings", although they considered that by design the O-rings would not be damaged. In fact it happened that they suffered some recurrent damage. The first time the O-rings were damaged the engineers found a solution and decided the space transportation system to be flying with "acceptable risk". The second time damage occurred, they thought the trouble came from something else. Because in their mind they believed they fixed the newest trouble, they again defined it as an acceptable risk and just kept monitoring the problem. And as they recurrently observed the problem with no consequence they got to the point that flying with the flaw was normal and acceptable. Of course, after the accident, they were shocked and horrified as they saw what they had done.

> As they recurrently observed the problem with no consequence they got to the point that flying with the flaw was normal and acceptable.

Challenger and *Columbia* Were Lost for the Same Reason

You indicate the O-Ring problem for Challenger *(1986). But in the CAIB [Columbia Accident Investigation Board] report in 2003 you write that it was the same situation for* Columbia. *However the technological reason was different that time.*

The causes of the two accidents were identical. In one case they flew with O-ring problems that they considered

At mission control in Houston, Texas, spacecraft communications personnel Frederick Gregory (right) and Richard O. Covey watch as the *Challenger* breaks apart during takeoff. (© Space Frontiers/Hulton Archive/Getty Images.)

were not a risk to flight safety, and the more they flew the more they demonstrated that the problem had no consequences. For *Columbia* they flew with foam debris that hit the heat shield of the orbiter wing [during lift off] and removed some tiles from it and the more they observed such debris hits the more they considered that they had no safety consequences. Tile damage was defined as a maintenance problem only. Each time they replaced the heat tiles and it was ready to go again. So the outcome was that one day at *Columbia* reentry into the earth's atmosphere the orbiter broke into parts . . . and the flight data indicated that foam debris hits on the wing at the moment of launch had created a large hole in the wing. The heat of reentry started a fire and the shuttle disintegrated. So, as I indicate in papers and in the CAIB report we have 2 technical situations, very different in terms of technology but identical in terms of social normalization of deviance. Exactly the same: in both cases, there was a history of early warning signs that were misinterpreted or ignored until it was too late.

Well, space transportation is a dangerous task and statistics are known to be poorly reliable for "small numbers", and somehow the number of launches is low compared to the number of commercial flights . . . So aren't we passing judgement on tragic events that somehow must happen from time to time . . . the history of mankind gives some evidences to this dramatic reality?

> One of NASA's failings was to treat space flight as routine and operational, when in fact it was and will continue to be experimental.

Yes, you make a very good point. One of NASA's failings was to treat space flight as routine and operational, when in fact it was and will continue to be experimental. NASA failures, though rare, are dramatic and have enormous political consequences, as well as costing billions of dollars. So it becomes important for many reasons to find out what happened. Blame must be placed so the program can continue. But in these two accidents are data indicating that other organizations fail for the same reasons. So something is to be gained from research investigating causes of accidents. In particular, the idea of early warning signs that are missed, but also that elite decisions about resources and goals keep employees at the lower level moving forward, normalizing deviance time after time.

Early Warning Signs of Trouble Are Generally Ignored

"Early signs". . . this seems to be a concept you are fond of . . . not that it appears only in The Challenger Launch Decision *but also as early as in the publication of [the book]* Uncoupling: Turning Points in Intimate Relationships. *Any comments?*

If you think about it, the idea of early warning signs and missed, weak, and routine signals that are ignored contribute to many kinds of harmful outcomes. In 1978, sociologist Barry Turner wrote a book called *Man-Made Disasters*, in which he examined 85 different accidents and found that in common [they] had a long incubation period with warning signs that were not taken seriously. Now we read that in the dramatic school shootings in the United States, that preceding the moment when the students went into the schools with guns, were many signals that they were angry, alienated, and planning a dangerous act. When the US was attacked on September 11, 2001, the entire country was shocked and surprised. But the 9/11 investigating commission discovered that the terrorist attack too was preceded by a history of early warning signs that were misinterpreted or ignored. Whether talking about failed relationships or terrorist attacks, the ignorance of what is going on is organizational and prevents any attempt to stop the unfolding harm. An important distinction between relationships failure and shuttles exploding, corporate misconduct, and terrorist attacks is politics and the decisions of elites who set problems in organizations in motion.

> Missed, weak, and routine signals that are ignored contribute to many kinds of harmful outcomes.

Challenger *blew up in 1986 and you published in 1996, I mean 9 to 10 years after.*

It took about 9 years to come to the final version. When I started, it was from the point of view that it was misconduct. I kept looking for "rule violations", but I didn't find any. In fact engineers conformed to rules and doing so normalized the deviance. After about a year I had to throw everything out and start over. It has been a long process to understand why and how they normalized deviance. I relied on thousands of documents in the US National Archives that were placed there by the government investigation. Many of these were engineering documents and memos. Doing the research involved learning engineering and NASA language. In the *Challenger* case there is this notion of "levels" of "acceptable risk", for example. These were called "Criticality Levels." Each part on the shuttle had to be classified at a Criticality level, meaning the probability of failure. Same for *Columbia*. NASA's risk assessment procedures were very complicated. The reality was that every attempt they made to quantify and clarify risk gave them no help because there were thousands of technical components on the shuttle. Instead of clarifying, it was just overwhelming—for NASA engineers and managers doing the risk assessments and for me, doing the research!

Was your work very welcome at the time of publishing?

Yes, beyond anything I had imagined. *The Challenger Launch Decision* was published for the 10th anniversary of the *Challenger* accident. The timing brought it much more attention than if it had been published earlier. On the anniversary day, it was reviewed by more than 40 newspapers over the nation. I was credited for a lot of inventions. It was a thick, dense and very technical book and I never thought it would be read by so many people.

Congress Blamed NASA for Several Years of Poor Technical Management

Don Fuqua

After the report of the Rogers Commission on the Challenger accident was published, a congressional committee also investigated the accident. It agreed with the report on most points, but unlike the commission, it concluded that the underlying problem was not just poor communication or inadequate procedures but poor decision-making by both NASA and contractor managers over a long period of time. Information about the flaws in the solid rocket booster joints had been available to managers at all levels, and they had not recognized that the problem was serious. They were in no hurry to correct it. Furthermore, the congressional committee identified other problems with the space shuttle program that the Rogers Commission did not address, and the committee was not confident that NASA had enough technical expertise to solve them. However, it strongly supported future continuation of manned space flight. Don Fuqua was a US congressman from Florida and chairman of the investigation of the Challenger accident by the US House of Representatives Committee on Science and Technology.

SOURCE. Don Fuqua, "Conclusions," Investigation of the Challenger Accident, US House of Representatives.

NASA management and the Congress must re-member the lessons learned from the *Challenger* accident and never again set unreasonable goals which stress the system beyond its safe functioning.

The Committee commends the work of the Rogers Commission and its supporting panels at NASA. Their investigation and the reports that document their efforts are very broad in scope and exceptionally detailed considering the time that was available to accomplish their task.

As a rule, the Committee agrees with the findings reached by the Rogers Commission. However, there are areas where the Committee either disagrees with a Rogers Commission finding or with the relative importance that the Rogers Commission attached to that finding.

Like the Rogers Commission, the Committee concluded that the *Challenger* accident was caused by a failure in the aft field joint on the right-hand Solid Rocket Motor. Additionally, we agree with the Rogers Commission that this tragic accident was not caused by the Orbiter, the Space Shuttle Main Engines, the External Tank, the onboard payloads, the ground support equipment, or the other elements of the Solid Rocket Boosters [SRBs]. We also agree that the failure of the joint was due to a faulty design, and that neither NASA nor Thiokol fully understood the operation of the joint prior to the accident. Further, the joint test and certification programs were inadequate, and neither NASA nor Thiokol responded adequately to available warning signs that the joint design was defective.

In concurrence with the Rogers Commission, the Committee confirms that the safety, reliability, and quality assurance programs within NASA were grossly inadequate, but in addition recommends that NASA review its risk management activities to define a complete risk management program. The Committee also agrees that a thorough review must be conducted on all Criticality 1

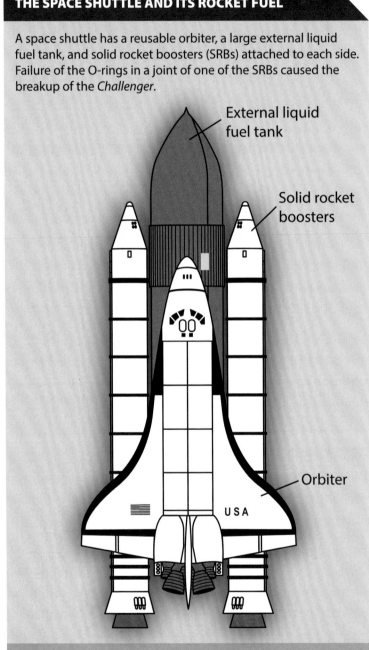

THE SPACE SHUTTLE AND ITS ROCKET FUEL

A space shuttle has a reusable orbiter, a large external liquid fuel tank, and solid rocket boosters (SRBs) attached to each side. Failure of the O-rings in a joint of one of the SRBs caused the breakup of the *Challenger*.

External liquid fuel tank

Solid rocket boosters

Orbiter

USA

Taken from: NASA, "Space Shuttle Drawing," Marshall Space Flight Center Image Exchange. http://mix.msfc.nasa.gov.

and 1R items and hazard analyses; a study should be conducted on how to provide Space Shuttle crews with a means of escape during controlled gliding flight; and NASA's Shuttle management structure, safety organization, communications procedures, and maintenance policies should be carefully scrutinized and improved.

In other areas, the Committee reached somewhat different conclusions than the Rogers Commission:

> The Rogers Commission concluded that NASA's decision-making process was flawed. The Committee does agree that the Marshall Space Flight Center should have passed along to higher management levels the temperature concerns that Thiokol engineers raised the night before the launch of Mission 51-L. However, the Committee feels that the underlying problem which led to the *Challenger* accident was not poor communication or inadequate procedures as implied by the Rogers Commission conclusion. Rather, the fundamental problem was poor technical decision-making over a period of several years by top NASA and contractor personnel, who failed to act decisively to solve the increasingly serious anomalies in the Solid Rocket Booster joints.
>
> Information on the flaws in the joint design and on the problems encountered in missions prior to 51-L was widely available and had been presented to all levels of Shuttle management. Despite the presence of significant amounts of information and the occurrence of at least one detailed briefing at Headquarters on the difficulties with the O-rings, the NASA and Thiokol technical managers failed to understand or fully accept the seriousness of the problem. There was no sense of urgency on their part to correct the design flaws in the

'The fundamental problem was poor technical decision-making over a period of several years by top NASA and contractor personnel.'

SRB. No one suggested grounding the fleet, nor did NASA embark on a concerted effort to remedy the deficiencies in O-ring performance. Rather, NASA chose to continue to fly with a flawed design and to follow a measured, 27-month, corrective program. . . .

Issues Not Addressed by the Rogers Commission

In still other areas, the Committee has raised concerns that do not appear to have been addressed sufficiently by the Rogers Commission. We are concerned that:

- There are numerous other recurrent hardware problems that are either not fully understood by NASA or have not been corrected.

- The existing internal communication system is disseminating too much information, often with little or no discrimination in its importance. Accordingly, recipients have difficulty "separating the wheat from the chaff."

- Existing contract incentives used by NASA do not adequately address or promote safety and quality concerns—most emphasis is placed on meeting cost and schedule requirements.

- NASA does not yet understand how or why the deficiencies in Solid Rocket Motor testing and certification went undetected in spite of the very comprehensive processes and procedures used by the agency to conduct and oversee these activities. The Committee is concerned that without such an understanding, NASA will not be able to protect against a similar breakdown in its system of checks and balances in the future. . . .

- The Committee is not assured that NASA has adequate technical and scientific expertise to conduct

the Space Shuttle program properly. NASA has suffered staffing reductions in key areas over several years. Moreover, it loses a significant number of technical/scientific personnel due to an imbalance between the government salary schedule and that of the private sector. The salary structure also inhibits NASA's ability to recruit top technical talent to replace its losses. . . .

On July 14, 1986, NASA submitted to the President a report on what actions the space agency plans to take in response to the recommendations of the Rogers Commission. The Committee believes that the plans contained in this report are a step in the right direction. When fully implemented, these plans should substantially improve the safety of Space Shuttle flight

Don Fuqua (second from right), chairman of the House Science and Technology Committee, reviews a copy of the Presidential Shuttle Commission's report along with panel chairman William P. Rogers (second from left) and fellow committee members. (© **John Duricka/AP Images.**)

operations. The Committee also endorses NASA's decision to move the proposed date for the next Space Shuttle launch beyond June 1987. This is a realistic and responsible decision that has removed some unnecessary pressure from the government and contractor personnel who must ensure that all hardware will be in readiness to reinstitute safe flight operations. . . .

The Space Shuttle Program Should Continue

In closing, the Committee would like to state that it continues to believe in and remains committed to a vigorous civilian space program. The Committee also continues to believe that the Space Shuttle is a critically important element of that program. The Committee's purpose, as NASA's primary overseer in the House, must be to monitor, understand, and help correct where necessary the patterns in NASA which lead to weakened and ineffective operation.

We are at a watershed in NASA's history and the Nation's space program. NASA's 28-year existence represents its infancy. We must use the knowledge and experience from this time to insure a strong future for NASA and the U.S. space program throughout the 21st century.

This Committee has long been proud of the many awe-inspiring achievements of NASA and understands the importance of NASA's programs to the future well-being of this country. We as a Committee have perhaps exhibited the human inclination to accept the successful completion of a flight or event as an indication of the overall strength of all aspects of its planning and execution. Perhaps it is arrogant to dissect and interrogate relentlessly projects and programs that bring home repeated A's for achievement and accomplishment. However, all of us—NASA, the Committee, the Congress and the Nation—have learned from the *Challenger* tragedy that it is wisdom to do so, and it is a reflection of respect for the human fallibility that we all possess.

We have no doubt that through the hard work and dedication of the men and women at NASA and its supporting contractors, the Space Shuttle will be safely returned to flight status—and will once again continue to impress people around the world with its many important accomplishments.

As has been said many times since the January 28th [1986] tragedy, space flight is a high risk undertaking. The Committee accepts this fact and applauds those men and women who, in spite of this risk, have chosen manned space flight as a career. Though we grieve at the loss of the *Challenger* crew, we do not believe that their sacrifice was in vain. They would not want us to stop reaching into the unknown. Instead, they would want us to learn from our mistakes, correct any problems that have been identified, and then once again reach out to expand the boundaries of our experience in living and working in outer space.

> We have no doubt that through the hard work and dedication of the men and women at NASA and its supporting contractors, the Space Shuttle will be safely returned to flight status.

The Rocket Engineers' Warnings Against the Launch Were Wrongly Ignored

Mark Hayhurst

In the following viewpoint, a British TV producer and author details his interview with Roger Boisjoly, a rocket engineer for Thiokol, the company that built the solid rocket boosters for the *Challenger* space shuttle. Boisjoly warned against launching *Challenger* in cold weather because of possible failure of the O-ring seals. Boisjoly and another engineer worked on the shuttle's solid rocket booster and had seen damage to the O-rings after past flights. In a meeting the night before the launch, they argued strongly that it would be unsafe, but their protests were overridden by managers from their own company who wanted to please NASA by not insisting on further delay. Boisjoly watched the launch reluctantly because he expected trouble. Later, during the investigation, he testified before the Rogers Commission and provided documents

SOURCE. Mark Hayhurst, "'I Knew What Was About to Happen,'" *Guardian*, January 22, 2001. Copyright © 2001 by the Guardian. All rights reserved. Reproduced by permission.

showing that his warnings were ignored. After he testified he was resented, both by the company and by the community of which he had once been mayor. Mark Hayhurst was the producer of a British television special about *Challenger* that aired on the fifteenth anniversary of the disaster.

It is 15 years [as of 2001] since the space shuttle *Challenger* exploded 73 seconds after lifting off from Cape Canaveral, but the signature it left in the Florida skies remains vivid in the mind. It looked like a body writhing in agony. Out of a trunk of white cloud came two unfettered rockets, dementedly skywriting, like a pair of thrashing limbs attached to a decapitated torso. At the same time hundreds of burning fragments started to cascade to the ocean, leaving their own smoky entrails.

Rob Navias, a veteran radio reporter, was speaking the words most people felt: "Can it . . . Can it? Oh my God, can *Challenger* have exploded? Oh no!" "What on Earth has happened?" he added, intending no irony.

In stark terms the fireball in the sky was the result of half a million gallons of liquid fuel vapourising, but neither the NASA man nor Navias knew for sure what had happened.

No one knew for sure. But there were two men watching on a TV screen far away in Utah who had a pretty good idea. One was Roger Boisjoly, a senior engineer at Morton-Thiokol, the contractors that built the solid rocket boosters for the space shuttle. The other was his manager, Bob Ebeling.

A few minutes before the launch Boisjoly had been walking past Thiokol's conference room. Ebeling came rushing out and "grabbed my arm and asked me to come in and watch the launch. At first I told Bob, 'no, I don't want to see the launch'. I knew what was about to happen and I just did not want to see the failure".

The previous evening Boisjoly and Ebeling had spent six hours in teleconference with NASA managers arguing that the *Challenger* launch should be delayed. The two men had been told that the temperature in Florida was plummeting to below freezing and had been instantly concerned about whether their rockets would perform properly in such conditions.

> [Two Morton-Thiokol engineers] spent six hours in teleconference with NASA managers arguing that the *Challenger* launch should be delayed.

They appeared to be winning the argument—until their own managers turned against them and gave NASA the recommendation they appeared to want: to launch.

Boisjoly was persuaded by Ebeling to watch the TV that fateful morning of January 28, 1986. He sat on the floor in front of the screen, resting his back against the legs of the older man. When the clock reached T minus five seconds the two engineers held hands and braced themselves for an explosion. But to their immense relief *Challenger* cleared the launch pad. "I turned to Bob and said 'we've just dodged a bullet,' because it was our expectation it would blow up on the pad."

The two men began to relax. But then, at 73 seconds, the heart-stopping plume of white smoke suddenly filled the screen. "There was silence for the longest time," says Boisjoly. "Then I went to my office, sat facing the wall and tried to hold back my emotions."

The Role of the Rocket Boosters

Boisjoly is telling me this outside Thiokol's test plant beneath the Wasatch Mountains in northern Utah. He hasn't been here since leaving the company in July 1986, soon after testifying before the presidential commission into the *Challenger* disaster. His testimony, much praised by the commissioners, was heavily critical of his managers, and Boisjoly acquired a reputation as a whistleblower.

The company blamed him for releasing documents to the commission which they had not asked for and had no idea existed; his community, for whom he'd once been mayor, blamed him for putting precious jobs in jeopardy.

We're not welcome to go into the plant, but we can walk around the rocket park. It's a fantastic sight. The place bristles with 20 or so rocket motors, including half-remembered names such as the Minuteman, the Peacekeeper, and a Poseidon. The scene-stealer, though, is a decommissioned solid rocket booster hoisted on metal stanchions, 126 ft [38m] long and dwarfing everything else.

These provide nearly 75% of the thrust to get the shuttle into orbit and clearly, despite the disaster, they are still Thiokol's pride and joy. To commemorate his return, Boisjoly adds an entry to the apparently endless "cools"

Roger Boisjoly, an engineer from Morton-Thiokol, the company that built the rocket boosters for the doomed *Challenger* space shuttle, testifies before Congress in 1987. (© Duane Howell/ The Denver Post/Getty Images.)

and "far outs" in the visitors' book. "Roger Boisjoly," it reads, "I worked here and tried to stop the launch of *Challenger*."

Each booster gets filled with millions of pounds of solid propellant and sent down to Cape Canaveral. No railway can transport an object 126 ft [38m] long—at least none with a bend in. Thiokol had to build the rockets in sections and ship them to Florida, where they were reassembled on site.

Boisjoly explains what happens when the boosters are ignited. "The steel rim might look tough, but on ignition each section like this reacts to the intense pressure by blowing up like a balloon. When that happens something has to take up the slack where the joints are, to stop hot gas pouring out of the rocket."

That job was given to two quarter-inch rubber seals called O-rings, which had to expand with the metal and seal the gaps. If they failed to keep contact with the metal parts for more than a fifth of a second there would be a leakage. "When solid rocket boosters leak," concludes Boisjoly, "they explode."

> The tragedy of *Challenger* is that [Roger] Boisjoly had been airing doubts about the O-rings for at least six months before the disaster.

"On the day *Challenger* launched it was very cold," he says, "and when the temperatures dropped these rubber O-rings became harder and less pliable. Hard O-rings move slower and they seal less effectively. There might only be fraction of a second's difference but that is enough to separate success from total disaster."

Warnings of Trouble

The tragedy of *Challenger* is that Boisjoly had been airing doubts about the O-rings for at least six months before the disaster. A year earlier he'd gone to Florida to inspect the spent rockets from a previous mission. He had been

THE SOLID ROCKET BOOSTER'S O-RINGS

This diagram of a solid rocket booster (SRB) shows the location of the O-ring joint that failed in the *Challenger*.

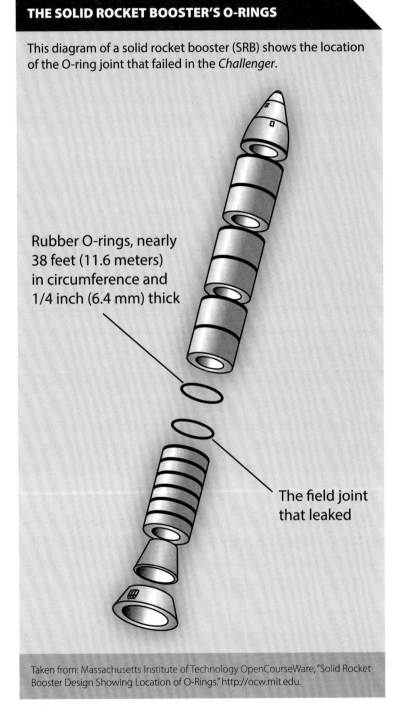

Rubber O-rings, nearly 38 feet (11.6 meters) in circumference and 1/4 inch (6.4 mm) thick

The field joint that leaked

Taken from: Massachusetts Institute of Technology OpenCourseWare, "Solid Rocket Booster Design Showing Location of O-Rings." http://ocw.mit.edu.

amazed at the condition of the joints. The primary seal had failed and allowed hot gas to surge by.

Fortunately the secondary O-ring had trapped the gas. He shows me a photograph he took of the burned joint. All around the seals the normally honey-coloured grease has turned jet black, and parts of the primary O-ring are missing—clear signs that the joint has been scorched. "When I saw that, I almost had a cardiac arrest," says Boisjoly. "I could not believe that we had not blown the shuttle up."

NASA put the O-rings on the critical list. Thiokol created a task-force to look into the problem, but a shortage of equipment and personnel meant little was accomplished. Boisjoly, a task-force member, sent a memo to Thiokol's vice-president, pleading for a greater sense of urgency in testing the O-rings. "It is my honest and very real fear," he wrote, "that if we do not take immediate action . . . we stand in jeopardy of losing a flight, along with all the launch pad facilities. The result would be a catastrophe of the highest order—loss of human life."

That was July 31, 1985. On the same day, on the Johnny Carson show, America was being introduced to the most recent recruit to the astronaut elite. Her name was Christa McAuliffe. She wasn't an astronaut really. She was a schoolteacher who had beaten off 11,000 other teachers to win a place on a forthcoming shuttle mission.

Alongside Carson she was impressively unflappable, as if to "the right stuff" born, but she also showed a very un-astronaut ability to see the funny side to what she was about to do. She laughed when her host said that as a kid there were several teachers he would have just lo-o-o-o-ved to have sent into space.

I went to see Christa's mother, Grace Corrigan, who lives in Framingham, Massachusetts. Her husband, Ed, died 10 years ago, retaining a deep anger at NASA to the end of his life. Grace is a smart, good-looking woman with eyes that dance when she speaks. She has a huge oil painting of Christa in her blue astronaut suit, cradling in her arms a model of *Challenger*. "Everybody was on a high," she says recalling the moment Christa was first chosen to become the teacher-in-space. "It was just one of those nice things that happens to nice people. And everywhere she went they just rolled out the red carpet for her. She didn't come on strongly or anything. People just accepted her."

The Launch Was Postponed

Challenger was meant to launch on January 25, but was twice postponed because of adverse weather reports. Then it was put back yet again, farcically this time. The astronauts were strapped into their seats and preparing for the final countdown when the close-out crew found they couldn't take the handle off the door because one of the screws had a broken thread.

A drill was found but a succession of batteries were flat. Finally, after five hours, a hacksaw was used to sever the bolt and the door was closed. But crosswinds had built to unacceptable levels. The launch was scrubbed again.

Grace followed some of this from her place in the grandstands. The irritation, and the sense that it still might be otherwise, remains strong today. "I mean, after all, this is NASA, right? They can do all these great things. They can launch, they can put a ship up in orbit. And they can't fix a screw on a handle!"

That afternoon the temperature at the Cape began to plummet. The launch team needed specialist advice. At around 6pm the call was made to Utah to ask whether Morton-Thiokol had any concerns about launching their rockets at a predicted −5°C (23°F). When the answer was "yes" another call was put in, this time to NASA's rocket specialists at the Marshall space flight centre in Huntsville, Alabama.

Judson Lovingood at the shuttle projects office received the call, and set about contacting his own engineers. I arranged to meet him in the room that he'd been in that night when the teleconference finally got under way. On the wall are the shields of all the shuttle missions NASA has flown, including the *Challenger* flight of January 1986: the only one without a date of re-entry.

He describes in unnerving detail who was there and where everyone sat and his eyes begin to fill—which is ironic, since he's been relating how he was a product of the very special, unsentimental, culture which prevailed here. If an engineer began a sentence starting with "I know" he was listened to with respect. If he began with an "I think," he never got to complete the first sentence. "You don't do engineering by emotion," Lovingood explains. "You can't get up and say, 'Hey, I've got a gut feeling this thing's gonna blow up.' They'll take you to the funny farm."

A Fatal Decision

That night the men at Marshall did listen to Boisjoly and his colleagues from Morton-Thiokol as they explained why the launch shouldn't go ahead in the morning. But they felt that what they were hearing were gut reactions, not engineering rationales. There was data, plenty of it, but it wasn't decisive, says Lovingood.

Thiokol's bottom line was that it didn't want to fly outside its data base—which meant not launching below 12°C (53°F), the coldest launch temperature to date, and the temperature responsible, according to Boisjoly, for the damaged joints he had inspected a year before. After nearly five hours a curious impasse had been reached, with NASA saying it wouldn't launch against a contractor's recommendation, but that the recommendation was baseless.

It was at this point that a Thiokol vice-president asked to go off-line for five minutes. Boisjoly says that "as soon as the button was pressed on the teleconference to sever us and mute us from NASA, our general manager Jerry Mason said in a soft voice that we had to make a 'management decision'. My whole being just started to rev up real bad because it was obvious that they were going to change from a 'no launch' to a 'go for launch' decision to accommodate their major customers."

It took 30 minutes, not five, but that is what happened. The engineers, including Boisjoly, were disenfranchised and the four senior managers voted to launch. Boisjoly stood up, grabbed the photograph of the burned O-rings, and planted it on the table in front of the four men. They refused to look at the photo. His boss released the mute button and told NASA that Thiokol had changed its mind. They were for launch.

> 'It was obvious that [Morton-Thiokol senior managers] were going to change from a "no launch" to a "go for launch" decision to accommodate [NASA].'

NASA had spent half the evening interrogating Thiokol over its initial recommendation. But this one provoked absolutely no debate. "That was a mistake," says Lovingood. "We should have asked them why they'd changed their minds." Instead Thiokol was simply asked to put its altered position into writing. It took a while to fax the new recommendation through to the Cape, but by midnight NASA had the "go" it needed to launch *Challenger* in the morning.

The Tragic Aftermath

Challenger of course didn't blow up once. It kept blowing up—all day long, all week long even. In a state of shock, Americans wanted to see it again and again, as if the networks' looped tapes could somehow unravel their own anxiety. Eventually the TV stations replaced the image of the stricken craft with more "positive" shots of the astronauts eating breakfast together on the morning of the launch, but as intelligence grew about what had gone wrong—and the sheer avoidability of it—these pictures became in turn like watching a condemned man eating a last meal.

Grace Corrigan accepts risk is an inherent part of spaceflight. It is hubris—and its strange bedfellow, complacency—she warns against. "We'd put NASA on a pedestal," she says. "We were all children of the first space age and we thought they could do no wrong. Since then we've been forced to grow up."

Boisjoly's disillusionment is greater. Corporate America dislikes a whistleblower and he has struggled to find work as an engineer since he walked away from Thiokol. For several years he was a wreck. "I beat myself up for a long time over what happened on that night. Maybe I hadn't done enough. Maybe I should have gone home and called the *New York Times* or something. Well, I don't beat myself up any more. If I couldn't convince the guys on the inside who know all the technical data, how would I have convinced total strangers? They would have called NASA and the PR people would have said, 'oh come on fellas, there hasn't been a launch since the start of space flight where some engineer hasn't tried to throw a switch and stop it.'"

If there is consolation for Boisjoly it is that since 1986, greater powers have been given to engineers working in, and for, NASA to express dissent and call off flights. Too late to save him, and too late to save *Challenger*, but a victory of sorts.

Many Factors Affected the Launch Decision and All Participants Had Regrets

Richard Kunz

In the following viewpoint, an engineer explains the combination of circumstances that led to the *Challenger* disaster, saying that no single factor was responsible for it. The launch had already been postponed twice—the recommendation of the engineers to postpone it again because of cold weather was overturned; unusual winds caused exceptionally low temperatures at the rocket booster's joints, yet management was not told of this; and one of the joints leaked during ignition but resealed, then reopened because of the severe wind shear. None of the people involved should be called heroes or villains, the author says; they were just human beings suddenly faced with a situation they had not met before, and all of them regretted that they had not acted differently.

SOURCE. Richard Kunz, "The Challenger Disaster: Making It Personal," *Proceedings of the 2011 ASEE Southeastern Section Conference*, April 2011. Copyright © 2011 by American Society for Engineering Education. All rights reserved. Reproduced by permission.

Richard Kunz is an associate professor of mechanical engineering at Mercer University School of Engineering in Macon, Georgia. He worked for fifteen years at Thiokol Corporation, beginning after the *Challenger* disaster, and became acquainted with some of the engineers and managers involved.

Most of us who were living on the morning of January 28, 1986 remember exactly where we were and what we were doing when we first learned of the explosion of the Space Shuttle *Challenger* 74.6 seconds into its flight. The public at large were shocked and saddened by the unexpected disaster. NASA at the time was widely considered to be infallible. Coming off the successful Apollo program of the late '60s and early '70s that sent men to the moon, the Space Shuttle program was touted as capable of providing routine, inexpensive access to space. The *Challenger* tragedy led to a very public re-examination of all aspects of Shuttle technology and the management culture at NASA and its contractors. The blue-ribbon Rogers Commission, appointed by President [Ronald] Reagan, held televised hearings aimed at identifying the root causes of the accident. Congressional hearings likewise investigated the accident. In the meantime, the Shuttle program was suspended for two-and-a-half years as all major systems and subsystems were re-evaluated, tested, and re-designed.

Many Unusual Circumstances Contributed to the Disaster

Although the technical cause of the failure is fairly clear-cut, the reasoning behind the decision to launch in the face of known or unknown technical risks has been the subject of innumerable books, papers, and reports. Did the engineers at NASA and at Morton-Thiokol, Inc. (the contractor responsible for the design and manufacture of the solid rocket boosters) fail to identify a clear temperature limitation on the operation of the motors? Was there a failure on the part of engineers to adequately communicate to management the risks inherent in a cold-temperature launch, or a failure of management to properly disseminate the available technical information? Were the program management systems in place inadequate to deal with a system as technologically complex as Shuttle? Had NASA begun to believe its own public relations department: that human space travel could be made routine, inexpensive, and free of risk? Had a culture of arrogance crept into the management at NASA and its contractors, and with it the belief that they could do no wrong? Did political and economic factors override good engineering judgment? Was everyone involved simply the victims of bad luck? In point of fact, all of the above likely played a role in the tragedy:

- The January 28 launch date was the third attempt to launch this flight of *Challenger*. The liftoff originally scheduled for January 26 was scrubbed due to a forecast of severe rain during the launch window; the weather that day turned out sunny and beautiful. The launch was rescheduled for the next day, but delayed when technicians were unable to remove the external handle of the door to the crew compartment. By the time the sticking handle was removed with a hacksaw, the launch window was closing and the weather had deteriorated as a cold front was coming through.

- The evening of January 27, as temperatures dropped and the forecast called for below-freezing air temperatures at launch, a teleconference was held between Morton-Thiokol and NASA personnel to review data on the effect of cold temperatures on the O-rings in the solid rocket boosters. Thiokol's engineers recommended no launch if the temperature of the O-rings was below 53°F. Their recommendation was overturned.

- Just prior to launch, an Ice Team typically measures the thickness of ice on the external tank with an infrared camera. This is a routine inspection; due to cryogenic liquids in the external tank, ice forms on its surface even in summer. By chance, the Team recorded a temperature of 8°F at the aft field joint of the right booster. Post-flight analysis indicated that unusual sustained WNW [west-northwest] winds caused the air to be supercooled as it flowed over the external tank and to impinge on the aft field joint directly facing the external tank. The unusually low temperature recorded at the joint was not passed up through the management chain because it was the Ice Team's responsibility only to estimate the thickness of the ice.

- During the ignition transient, the right aft field joint leaked facing the external tank, but then resealed after a few seconds as motor pressure built up. At 58 seconds into launch, the Shuttle passed through the most severe wind shear recorded on any flight to date, causing the booster to flex and reopening the leak. By chance, the leak impinged directly on the attach strut and the external tank itself, leading to catastrophic failure.

Photo on previous page: The *Challenger* is shrouded in mist on the morning of its fateful launch in January of 1986. The below-freezing temperatures were credited as a contributing factor in the explosion. (© **Space Frontiers/Getty Images.**)

If any one of the above scenarios had played out even slightly differently, it is likely that the *Challenger* launch would have proceeded without incident, and the crew would have returned home safely. As it was, a very public tragedy occurred, and the effects on NASA, the aerospace engineering industry, and the public trust were profound. Since then, studies and analyses of the events surrounding the *Challenger*

> If any one of the scenarios had played out even slightly differently, it is likely that the *Challenger* launch would have proceeded without incident.

accident have become a mainstay of college curricula. Corresponding issues of engineering ethics and the breakdown of technical communication have routinely been discussed on college campuses nationwide for many years. . . .

The Role of the Teleconference

The teleconference held the evening preceding the launch came to play a prominent role in the testimony before the Rogers Commission, and has been thoroughly documented in the final report issued by the Commission. . . .

The three-way conference call included engineers and managers from NASA and Thiokol in three different time zones.

- At Kennedy Space Center in Florida, [Allan] McDonald from Thiokol, along with Larry Mulloy, NASA Marshall Space Flight Center (MSFC) Solid Rocket Booster Project Manager, and Stan Reinartz, MSFC Shuttle Project Manager.

- At MSFC in Huntsville, Alabama, George Hardy, Deputy Director of Science and Engineering, along with a team of NASA engineers.

- At the Thiokol plant in northern Utah, engineering members of the O-ring task force, including Arnie Thompson, Brian Russell, and Roger Boisjoly; Robert Lund, Thiokol's Vice-President of Engineering; and Thiokol senior executives Joe Kilminster, VP of Space Booster Programs; Cal Wiggins, VP and General Manager of the Space Division; and Jerry Mason, Senior VP of Wasatch Operations.

Task force members had less than four hours to summarize their work in progress and prepare a presentation to NASA. In those days before widespread use of PCs and PowerPoint, Thiokol's handwritten presentation charts were faxed to Kennedy and Marshall. The Thiokol engineers, citing incomplete preliminary data, presented trends that indicated possible deleterious effects of cold temperatures on O-ring sealing effectiveness. Discussion of the data among the participants lasted over an hour until 10:00 PM ET [eastern time]. The conclusions and recommendations, presented by Lund, specified a minimum O-ring temperature of 53°F at launch.

The NASA managers on the line were clearly not pleased with the recommendation. Hardy said that he was appalled by Thiokol's conclusion, but he would not fly without Thiokol's concurrence. Mulloy, noting that the data presented was inconclusive, blurted, "My God, Thiokol, when do you want me to launch, next April?" It should be noted that it was not unusual for NASA officials to question, sometimes very bluntly, the interpretation of data presented at formal Flight Readiness Reviews held before every launch, as well as at informal, ad hoc conferences such as this. But always in the past, it was up to Thiokol to prove to NASA's satisfaction that it was safe to fly. This was the first time in any of the Thiokol participants' experience that NASA had challenged a recommendation that it was unsafe to fly. In the past, data that was inconclusive was automatically rejected to support a launch recommendation.

Clearly rattled by the unexpected reaction by Thiokol's biggest customer Kilminster requested a five-minute off-line caucus by Thiokol personnel on the line in Utah. During the caucus, two of the engineers present, Boisjoly and Thompson, reiterated their objections to launch while acknowledging that the data were insufficient to prove that the O-rings would fail at low temperature. Mason, the Big Dog in the room, favored a launch recommendation, and upon pointed questioning received support from two of the other three senior managers present: Wiggins and Kilminster. Lund, VP of Engineering, remained non-committal. Knowing that a launch recommendation required concurrence from Engineering, Mason finally said to Lund, "Bob, it's time for you to take off your engineering hat and put on your management hat." Lund, under pressure from his superiors, finally agreed that the launch should proceed with none of the constraints originally recommended by Engineering.

At the conclusion of the five-minute off-line caucus (which had turned into a 30-minute caucus) Thiokol came back on the line and communicated its new recommendations to NASA in Florida and Huntsville. Hardy requested that Thiokol provide its launch recommendation in writing and signed by a responsible Thiokol official. This was also a first: NASA had never before requested a signed recommendation to launch after a Flight Readiness Review. McDonald, Thiokol's senior manager present in Florida, was not a party to the discussions in Utah during the caucus. Baffled by the turn-around, he refused to sign the launch recommendation. Kilminster in Utah agreed to provide the signature and fax it to Kennedy and Marshall. And the launch proceeded as scheduled.

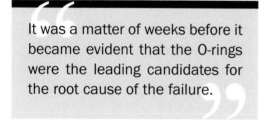

It was a matter of weeks before it became evident that the O-rings were the leading candidates for the root cause of the failure.

The Aftermath of the Disaster

The next morning, the tragic explosion of *Challenger* was met with horror and disbelief worldwide. Employees of NASA and the scores of Shuttle contractors across the country shared these emotions, along with a nagging burden of uncertainty: was it a system for which I am responsible that led to the failure? Certainly nowhere was this sense of unease and foreboding more pronounced than among the Thiokol participants in the teleconference. It was a matter of weeks before it became evident that the O-rings were the leading candidates for the root cause of the failure. Painstaking analysis of telemetry and photographic data along with on-board instrumentation and a detailed fault-tree analysis eventually led to the final conclusion. Many of the teleconference participants from both Thiokol and NASA were called upon to testify before the Rogers Commission and the Congressional panel. It is safe to say their lives, both professional and personal, were changed forever.

Whether reading detailed accounts or abbreviated case studies of the events leading up to the accident, it is tempting to assign labels of "villain" or "hero" to the participants. In point of fact, all involved were just human beings, many of them engineers or managers with engineering backgrounds, who were suddenly and unexpectedly put in a position none had ever been put in before. Some reacted differently than others, but it is safe to say that every one of them came out of it with life-long regrets that they did not do something differently that could have led to a different outcome. . . .

Of course, everything did not turn out all right [on January 28], and everyone in that conference room in Utah ended up replaying the 30 minutes of the offline caucus . . . over and over again. It is safe to say that each one of them has spent untold hours second-guessing himself and playing what-if games. But in fact, on the morning of January 27, 1986, not one of those individuals knew what was waiting for him that evening.

Manned space flight is inherently risky. Established margins of safety are lower than any other endeavor in which human lives are at stake. While it could be argued that if any one of a dozen scenarios had turned out slightly differently *Challenger* would not have exploded, it could equally be argued that the other Shuttle flights were one wrong decision away from disaster.

25 Years Later: How the *Challenger* Disaster Brought NASA Down to Earth

Traci Watson

In the following viewpoint originally published in January 2011, a journalist contends that the space program had reached "twilight status" and that some experts blame this on the *Challenger* disaster. President Ronald Reagan's promise that manned space flights would increase has not been fulfilled, she states. Some of what was learned from the accident was forgotten, resulting in the *Columbia* disaster of 2003, and other consequences continue to hold space exploration back. The author points out that space travel costs a lot of money, and funds have not matched goals. The shuttle could not do the jobs it was expected to do and was unable to make a profit from launching satellites. NASA's vigilance in detecting hazards did not last. And although most Americans still favor space flight despite the risks, the author maintains that even

SOURCE. Traci Watson, "25 Years Later: How the Challenger Disaster Brought NASA Down to Earth," *USA Today*, January 30, 2011. Copyright © 2011 by USA Today. All rights reserved. Reproduced by permission.

the next generation of ships will remain dangerous. Traci Watson is a writer for *USA Today*.

Twenty-five years ago Friday, the space shuttle *Challenger* vanished from the blue Florida sky, leaving only white corkscrews of smoke hanging in the air.

Challenger's disintegration 73 seconds after liftoff took the lives of high-school teacher Christa McAuliffe and six fellow astronauts, who perished in front of their families, friends and schoolchildren watching at Cape Canaveral and on live television across the nation.

Afterward, President Reagan told a shocked and grieving nation that the legacy of the accident would not be curtailed ambition for the space program, but accomplishments that would have made *Challenger's* crew proud.

A quarter-century later, however, that promise seems no more enduring than the smoke from *Challenger* that hovered over the Florida coast that chilly morning in January 1986. Some experts contend that the loss of *Challenger* gave America's human space program a significant push toward its twilight status today.

In the years after *Challenger*, America's human space program "has limped along," says Joan Johnson-Freese of the Naval War College in Newport, R.I., who has written several books about space policy. "There have been great plans that have been barely met, if at all."

The *Challenger* loss shrank America's fleet of shuttles from four to three, and forced important shuttle missions to be put on hold or canceled. As directed by President George W. Bush, NASA is about to retire the shuttle this year even though it has no replacement in the wings. NASA succeeded in building a huge space station in orbit, but proposals by various presidents to send crews to the moon and Mars have come to nothing.

Challenger's legacy is more complex than what Reagan hoped for. The accident taught NASA much about the vulnerabilities of the shuttle and how to make space travel safer, space specialists say.

However, some lessons from the accident eventually were forgotten, with a major consequence being the loss in 2003 of shuttle *Columbia*, which disintegrated on re-entry over Texas, killing seven astronauts.

The *Challenger* accident "was significant, because it set in train a whole set of changes at NASA," says Roger Launius, senior curator in space history at the Smithsonian's National Air and Space Museum. But eventually, "a kind of entropy sets in."

> Some lessons from the [*Challenger*] accident eventually were forgotten, with a major consequence being the loss in 2003 of shuttle *Columbia*.

That hardly seemed possible in 1986, when the accident plunged NASA into anguished soul-searching. Investigators appointed by Reagan found that NASA repeatedly had ignored serious technical problems. They criticized what they called NASA's "silent safety program" and "flawed" decision-making.

The investigators traced the specific cause of the accident to the shuttle's O-rings, rubbery seals in the two slender rocket boosters that flank the spacecraft. The defective O-rings allowed hot gases and flames to seep out, creating a blowtorch toward the spacecraft.

The investigators' findings led NASA to make a range of upgrades to the shuttle, which made the spacecraft safer—if not exactly safe. But other lessons from the accident continue to hang over the space agency.

1. Space Exploration Takes Big Bucks

After the accident, Congress poured money into NASA to fund its recovery from the catastrophe, including the construction of a shuttle to replace *Challenger*. NASA's budget soared from $15.5 billion (in 2010 dollars) in fiscal

Commitment to Space Has Declined Since the *Challenger* Disaster

At the dawn of the Space Age in the 1960s, people had strong emotions about space. It was often said, and widely believed, that becoming a spacefaring species was a major step forward in human evolution, and a base on Mars was sure to be established before the end of the century. No one then imagined that public apathy would cause progress in space to decelerate. Countless books and articles have speculated about why that happened, and opinions differ. Space advocates are puzzled and disheartened by it—even frightened if they believe humankind's future survival depends on not remaining confined to one small and vulnerable planet. Opponents, on the other hand, feel that the decreased attention given to space represents a more realistic assessment of values than existed in earlier decades. But on one thing nearly everyone agrees: ever since the successful moon landing, the US space program has lacked a clearly defined goal.

Is the chief long-term aim of space exploration to acquire scientific knowledge? To meet the human need for the challenge of frontiers? To utilize extraterrestrial energy and materials to replace the dwindling resources of Earth? To establish settlements on other worlds? To counter potential threats to national security posed by other nations' space capabilities? To develop readiness to deflect future natural catastrophes such as asteroid strikes? All of these goals have proponents, and to many, all are important—but there is no agreement, even among ardent space supporters, about which is the most vital or which should be given priority.

Over the years, the space shuttle program was increasingly criticized because it had no specific purpose. Though shuttles did significant work, critics pointed out that much of it could have been accomplished by unmanned spacecraft without endangering human lives. Many space advocates feel that the cost, effort, and risk involved made sense only if viewed as *preparation* for one or more envisioned long-term goals—and seen in that light, the shuttle missions achieved a great deal. Certainly the astronauts who took the risk had such a goal in mind. But the public did not, and there was no sense of urgency attached to what was being done in space, so bureaucracy gradually took over. That may be one reason why the loss of *Challenger* dimmed what was left of the widespread enthusiasm that prevailed during the Apollo era. People asked themselves why space travel is worth the sacrifices it demands, and many of them did not have an answer.

1986 to almost $21 billion the year after the accident, and it continued to trend upward for the next half-decade.

Since then, however, NASA often has faced "a disconnect between the goals that have been set and the funds that have been available to carry out those goals," says Norman Augustine, former chairman and CEO of Lockheed Martin who led a panel appointed by the Obama administration to examine NASA's plans.

One of the most recent victims of NASA's financial woes was a plan Bush announced in 2004 to return humans to the moon. In 2009, Augustine's panel concluded that there wouldn't be enough money, given NASA's existing budget, to pay for a new moonshot until the 2030s, "if ever." President Obama moved to cancel the effort in 2010. He told NASA to rely on private space companies to blast astronauts into space and to decide in 2015 on the design for a new, heavy-duty rocket that could blast humans to the moon and beyond.

Obama's new program didn't outlive the year. In September, Congress piled expensive new chores on NASA: Develop a new space pod to carry humans into orbit and beyond, build the big new rocket by 2017 and continue with some of Obama's pet projects, such as subsidies for private space companies.

Congress' to-do list "is not executable . . . in today's budgetary climate," says Marcia Smith, who runs SpacePolicyOnline.com. "The debate's going to continue on what this nation is actually going to fund."

NASA appears to agree. In a report the agency sent to the Congress this month, NASA officials wrote that neither of the preliminary designs for the new rocket and space pod that Congress wants "currently fits the projected budget profiles nor the schedule goals outlined" by lawmakers.

The new Republican leadership of the House of Representatives has promised to slash government funding, and NASA will make a tempting target, space analysts say.

The reality is that "this is all very expensive and you can't do everything," says Johnson-Freese, but that reality is one that "Congress is still not acknowledging. . . . We're setting ourselves up for another round of disappointment."

2. The Shuttle Couldn't Sustain a Business Plan

Starting in the 1970s, NASA billed the shuttle as a sturdy space truck that would haul satellites to orbit as routinely as postal trucks deliver the mail. The shuttle was supposed to fly several dozen missions a year, a number that was "pure fantasy," says political scientist Roger Handberg of the University of Central Florida.

The *Challenger* accident opened America's eyes to the shuttle's fragility and perils. After the tragedy the shuttle quickly was stripped of one of its primary occupations, the delivery of commercial satellites to space.

> Some [space scholars] argue that the nation's hard-earned knowledge of the shuttle's weaknesses changed the course of the space program.

Many space scholars think the accident can't be held accountable for NASA's plight today. But some argue that the nation's hard-earned knowledge of the shuttle's weaknesses changed the course of the space program.

If *Columbia*'s disintegration in 2003 had been the first loss of a shuttle rather than the second, "President Bush might have made a different decision on whether to keep the shuttle flying," says former astronaut Jay Apt, who joined NASA shortly before the *Challenger* accident and now is a professor at Carnegie Mellon University in Pittsburgh.

NASA had hoped the shuttle program would turn a profit through its income from launching private and

People watch footage of the space shuttle *Columbia* disintegrating during re-entry on February 1, 2003. NASA critics say that the agency should have heeded more of the lessons from the *Challenger* disaster seventeen years earlier. (© Bluefield Daily Telegraph/Eric DiNovo/AP Images.)

military satellites into space, which could be used to build a space station and research vehicles to get humans to the moon and Mars.

"When the shuttle turned out to be not what we thought it was, all those downstream visions began to crumble," says Howard McCurdy, a specialist in space policy at American University in Washington, D.C. "The business model collapsed, and it wasn't just the business model for shuttle, it was the business model for shuttle, station, Mars, the moon. . . . It was like a corporation going down."

3. Complacency Is Hard to Avoid

The accident sparked a frenzy of self-improvement efforts at NASA. Following the advice of Reagan's investigators, officials set up a new NASA-wide safety office.

Top NASA executives lost their jobs. Engineers redesigned the O-ring joints and added a bailout system for the crew's use in an emergency.

For a while, the agency was supremely vigilant for lurking hazards. The vigilance didn't last.

On Feb. 1, 2003, shuttle *Columbia* disintegrated just a few minutes before its scheduled landing in Florida. Investigators found that during liftoff, a chunk of foam insulation had peeled off the shuttle's 15-story fuel tank and bashed a massive hole in the shuttle's wing.

Investigators also learned that before the accident, large chunks of foam had fallen off the tank during a half-dozen missions. But engineers gradually accepted foam loss as routine, just as they had gradually accepted O-ring damage as routine.

Changes made after the shuttle's first fatal accident were "undone over time," *Columbia* investigators wrote, adding that they "had a hard time understanding how, after the bitter lesson of *Challenger*, NASA could have failed to identify a similar trend."

"People retire, and we lose some of the corporate memory," says former astronaut Rick Hauck, who commanded the first shuttle mission after *Challenger*. "We become less sensitive to issues we were more sensitive to in proximity to the failures."

"We had let our guard down," says Bryan O'Connor, an astronaut at the time of the *Challenger* accident and now NASA's top safety official. "It's so human to become complacent."

4. "There Will Be Accidents"

Before *Challenger*, NASA made spaceflight look easy and safe—safe enough to allow a schoolteacher to fly on the shuttle. The accident was a reminder that space exploration will, at one time or another, cost lives.

Americans decided they could accept that cost. Public support for NASA and the shuttle program in the months just after the shuttle's loss ran 70% to 80%, Launius says.

The public still overwhelmingly supports the astronaut program. A survey taken in October by polling firm Rasmussen Reports found 72% of respondents said it was at least somewhat important for the nation to have a human space program.

> The public still overwhelmingly supports the astronaut program.

After *Challenger*, Americans understood "that there is risk to human spaceflight," Smith says. "But that was not enough to deter us from continuing our quest for space exploration."

That tolerance for loss of life is likely to be tested again as long as humans continue to blast into space, many space experts say.

The problem is that any craft blasting into space has to go from a standstill to 17,000 mph, the speed needed to orbit the Earth, says O'Connor, NASA's safety chief. That requires a huge and dangerous jolt of power. Even all the private companies now designing spaceships can't avoid that uncomfortable truth.

The ideas for the "next generation of spaceflight vehicles continue, in my opinion, to be high risk," O'Connor says. "Getting up and back is the hardest thing, and, oh, by the way, while you're up there it's not that benign either."

"Spaceflight, like landing aircraft on aircraft carriers at night, is fundamentally dangerous," says Terence Finn, a former NASA shuttle official. "There will be accidents along the way."

Nothing Ventured

Bob Barr

In the following viewpoint, a US congressman writes in late 2002 that the United States has become unwilling to accept the risks of space exploration. At the time of the space program's first tragedy—the 1967 fire during a ground test of the Apollo 1 space capsule—the problem was quickly fixed and the program continued. The *Challenger* disaster, less than a generation later, was handled very differently; the space program came to a halt for nearly three years and alterations were made on the basis of fear. The United States used to welcome challenges, the author says, but by the twenty-first century it had lost boldness and confidence. In the author's opinion, the fundamental cause of the space program's decline is the lack of vision on the part of leaders. People no longer take pride in achievement against odds, he argues, and they are squandering the legacy of past space successes. Bob Barr is a former member of the US House of Representatives and was the 2008 presidential nominee of the Libertarian Party.

Contrary to the knowledge possessed by many Americans, whose view of the space program began with the 1986 *Challenger* explosion, that

SOURCE. Bob Barr, "Nothing Ventured," *American Spectator,* January–February 2003. Copyright © 2003 by the American Spectator. All rights reserved. Reproduced by permission.

Photo on following page: The charred remains of the practice module for the Apollo I mission are examined at NASA in 1967. A fire in the pod killed three astronauts, marking NASA's first major accident resulting in astronaut death. (© MPI/Getty Images.)

tragedy was not the American space program's first. Its predecessor occurred nineteen years earlier, almost to the day—the Apollo I fire, January 27, 1967. The differing manner in which our nation responded to these tragedies—and the resulting effects on the U.S. space program—speak volumes about the America of the 1960s and the nation now facing the challenges of this new millennium.

Following the Apollo I fire—which claimed the lives of three brave astronauts, Gus Grissom, Roger Chaffee, and Ed White—the government immediately began an investigation, determined the cause of the tragedy, fixed the problem, and launched the first successful Apollo capsule, just nine months later. In short, we did not drown ourselves in prolonged self-pity, nor did we change our approach to the world. We dealt with the situation by picking ourselves up, dusting ourselves off, fixing the problem, moving on, and not looking back.

Less than a generation later, we handled the *Challenger* explosion in a very different manner. Amid protracted mourning and flagellation, the entire space program came to a grinding halt. The Shuttle program was halted entirely for nearly three years, and other aspects of our space program were dramatically altered simply because we feared there might be another explosion in the future. That's how little faith we had in our own capabilities. All this, even though the actual cause of the *Challenger* explosion was quickly determined to a high degree of certainty.

The America of four decades ago was bold and brave, actually relishing the risks of new endeavors and equal to any challenge man or nature might throw at us. The America of twenty years later—and even more so now, in 2002—was a nation unsure of its strength or its resolve to

> The America of four decades ago was bold and brave, actually relishing the risks of new endeavors and equal to any challenge man or nature might throw at us.

use it, always looking for the least-risky option, whether in war or peace. Indeed, were a U.S. president today to restate John F. Kennedy's bold "We will send a man to the moon and return him safely to the earth within the decade," few would listen, much less believe it could be done.

Recently I visited the John F. Kennedy Space Center in Florida for a Space Shuttle launch. Actually, a proposed Shuttle launch—it was scrubbed at the last minute, not because a serious problem had suddenly developed, but rather because a minor glitch was noted—something that "could possibly" be a problem. This is not my inexpert opinion—it was how the space center's head described it.

You want to know the level of fear in which NASA employees operate? At the Kennedy Space Center, warning signs pasted on doors leading to the outside world advise: "DO NOT GO OUTSIDE IF THERE IS LIGHTNING!" Remember, this is Florida, where nary a day goes by without some chance of lightning.

The touchy-feely era of America's space program has arrived. The ceremony leading to the aborted Shuttle launch was classic, modern-day America political correctness. Instead of the wonders of science and the challenges of space, we were treated to an Indian dance (hopefully not rain), a song by 1960s recording artist Buffy St. Marie (still a fine singer, but hardly a reason to go to a space launch), and a program focused on cute anecdotes about the Shuttle crew. One crew member was canonized simply because some of his ancestors are American Indian.

Apollo XIII's slogan—made famous in the movie of the same name—was "Failure is not an option." For NASA today, it should be, "Risk is not an option."

How did we get to this point? Much of it, counterintuitively, may be the result of our being the only superpower left. There is no one and nothing to challenge us.

So we constantly invent phony challenges—we manufacture boogey men, so to speak. Instead of giant leaps for mankind, we take halting baby steps, afraid of our shadow.

We could, for example, fairly easily and quickly neutralize the challenge that is Saddam Hussein. Yet we dither here and yon, fretting over how we will be perceived by superpower wannabes, or by that most bloated and irrelevant of bureaucracies, the United Nations—as if their approval meant something.

> Instead of giant leaps for mankind, we take halting baby steps, afraid of our shadow.

One of the most startling things about the Kennedy Space Center is the outwardly impressive Vehicle Assembly Building. Massive cranes and Rube Goldberg-type gantries hook boosters and Shuttles together—1950s technology, applied to a 1990s problem, in 2002. The guides told us proudly that "we" did it this way because that's the way it's always been done. It starts looking a lot less impressive.

You see this same approach to other problems. To waterproof the Shuttle's ceramic heat tiles, we were told—once again, with great pride—that before each launch, technicians in the VAB manually coat each and every one (there are thousands) with a Scotchguard-like substance. Otherwise, if it rains and the tiles absorb moisture, the entire spacecraft becomes too heavy to launch. (Note to NASA: it also rains in Florida.)

If we ran our military this way, we'd still be making carrier flight decks out of wood, but treating them with new and better water repellents than were available in the 1940s. And boasting about it.

Political correctness even creeps into the explanation of why we have a space program—as if meeting the challenges of space is something shameful. During our tour we were told—again, most proudly—that a major reason for the new space station was to "track" endangered species. No mention of mankind as endangered, if new resources are not found.

Yes, part of the problem is that neither the Congress nor successive presidents have put sufficient resources into the program. The fact is, however, without a constantly and aggressively articulated vision by our national leaders, the resources will not be made available because the case for their need is not being made.

> That magnificent legacy [of US achievements in space] is being squandered, lost in a sea of doubt, political correctness, and risk-aversion.

As a baby boomer who grew up marveling at the X-15, the Mercury astronauts, the Gemini explorers, and the Apollo giants, I remember the U.S. space program with unequaled pride—real pride in real achievement, against tremendous odds. But that magnificent legacy is being squandered, lost in a sea of doubt, political correctness, and risk-aversion. It is a blueprint for failure, not from a detour or a dead end. This is a more insidious type of failure—a dream unrealized, a door never opened, and a future never known.

CHAPTER 3

Personal Narratives

An Eyewitness Description of the *Challenger* Disaster on the Day It Happened

Bob Morris

Photo on previous page: Spectators watch as the space shuttle *Challenger* breaks apart over Cape Canaveral, Florida.   (© **Bettmann/ Corbis/AP Images.**)

In the following viewpoint, a reporter describes viewing the *Challenger* accident from the roof of a newspaper building. He describes a magnificent launch; all the observers thought the ship had a strange-looking vapor trail, he says, but he believed it was only the rocket stages separating normally. Then somebody heard on the radio that *Challenger* had exploded. Everyone rushed down to the newsroom and watched the tape play over and over. Two hours later, when he went back to the roof, the vapor trail was still visible, looking like a question mark in the sky. Bob Morris was a reporter for the *Orlando Sentinel*.

SOURCE. Bob Morris, "Coverage from the Day Space Shuttle Challenger Exploded: A Big Question Mark in the Sky," *Orlando Sentinel*, January 29, 1986. Copyright © 1986 by Orlando Sentinel. All rights reserved. Reproduced by permission.

It was a fine day for watching a liftoff—cold, but crisp and clear as could be.

A bunch of us gathered on the roof of the *Sentinel* to get a good look. We had gone up on the roof the day before, too, only to have the liftoff canceled thanks to bad weather and a fouled-up handle on the shuttle's hatch.

So after a couple of minutes just standing there Tuesday morning with nothing happening, the wisecracks began as expected.

"Another day, another delay," said someone.

"With a teacher on board you don't say it's late," said someone else. "It's tardy."

Someone shouted, "There it goes!" and jokingly pointed to the west, in the opposite direction of Cape Canaveral. Big joke. But you know how it goes with lift-offs. We've grown accustomed to them. And we've grown accustomed to them proceeding without any problems.

It wasn't always that way. In *The Right Stuff*, Tom Wolfe tells about the early, less-than-glorious days of our space program when the Russians were having all the luck. After numerous strikeouts, Wolfe wrote, the people at NASA started thinking: "Our rockets always blow up."

But after some 57 manned missions with hardly any post-launch incidents to speak of—the deaths of three astronauts in 1967 occurred in a fire before launch—we had every right to think: "Our rockets never blow up."

When we finally saw *Challenger* on Tuesday, it was big and blazing against a sky that was an almost impossible blue. No matter how many times you watch a liftoff—and I've watched more than I can count—you can't help but be awed by the magnificence of it all.

"God, look at it," said a woman standing next to me. "It's great."

I saw the explosion. But I really didn't think anything of it. Just thought it was one stage of the rocket separating as usual. But suddenly the one ball of fire we had been watching seemed to split into two parts that headed

Bystanders and photographers watch the launch of the *Challenger* space shuttle on January 28, 1986 from a VIP area at the Kennedy Space Center in Florida. (© Bruce Weaver/AP Images.)

in opposite directions. I figured one was *Challenger* and the other a booster rocket.

"Never seen it do that before," said someone.

"We're really sending up two rockets," said someone else. "It's one of those secret missions, only they didn't want us to know it was secret."

A Weird Vapor Trail

"What a weird vapor trail," said someone. "Looks like one of those inkblot tests a psychiatrist gives you."

A man standing behind me had a transistor radio.

"Explosion," I heard him say, softly at first. I turned around and saw him fiddling with his earplugs.

"There's been an explosion," he said, louder this time, and everyone on the roof drew toward him. He pulled the plugs from his ears and tried to turn up the radio so everyone could hear. But there was just static. The signal was weak. So he stuck the earplugs back in.

"It . . . blew . . . up," he said.

Everyone just stared at the sky for a moment. And then there was a rush from the roof, to the newsroom.

The next hour or so was crazy. And numbing. We watched the story unfold from Cape Canaveral on television. At first we thought the shuttle was coasting back to Earth. Then they said no, there had been confirmation of an explosion. There was a shot of someone descending in a parachute and we thought maybe, just maybe, one of the crew managed to escape. But no, it turned out to be a medic parachuting to the crash site.

> They played the tape of the launch and we all watched, sickened and chilled, as the awfulness of it all sank in.

They played the tape of the launch and we all watched, sickened and chilled, as the awfulness of it all sank in. They played that tape over and over. I don't care about ever seeing it again.

Two hours after it happened, I took a break and went back to the roof. The sky still was the most beautiful blue imaginable. To the west, a skywriter was doing his handiwork over Disney World, with smiley faces and a cheery "Hi!"

To the east, over Cape Canaveral, you could still see the vapor trail from *Challenger*. The contrail, they call it. And it looked like nothing so much as a big, white question mark in the sky.

Witnessing the Disaster from a Florida Schoolyard

Aaron Brame

In the following viewpoint, a teacher recalls witnessing the Challenger's *disintegration when he was in the third grade. It was an important event in his life: the day he first became aware of death. He was used to shuttle launches, because he lived in nearby Orlando, Florida, and his family always sat on their front lawn to watch. This launch occurred during school hours, however, and everyone in his class was excited because a teacher was aboard. When it was time, the whole class went out to the playground, but when they got there they could see that something terrible had happened. They knew enough about shuttles to realize what the strange cloud in the sky must mean. Aaron Brame is a teacher at the Memphis Academy of Science and Engineering, a charter preparatory school in Memphis, Tennessee.*

O f everything that ever happened to me as a child, nothing was as traumatic or meaningful as the explosion of the *Challenger* on January 28, 1986. It's an event that I have never been able to shake, and I find

SOURCE. Aaron Brame, "Where I Was When the Challenger Exploded," *Mr. Brame's Blog*, January 28, 2011. Copyright © 2011 by Aaron Brame. All rights reserved. Reproduced by permission.

myself returning to it at odd times, my thoughts drifting back to a cold morning when I was not yet nine years old. The *Challenger* disaster was my introduction to a world of chaos and unhappy endings, and it was such a crucial moment in my development as an individual that it seems impossible that it could have been witnessed by anybody else.

I didn't realize until this morning that today was the twenty-fifth anniversary of the event. At first I just blinked at the news, with a *what-do-you-know-about-that?* look on my face. But then I asked my students if they had ever heard of it, and of course they hadn't, so I showed them a clip from cnn.com. I was afraid they would snicker, or hoot, or say something crass when they watched the footage, but they didn't. They were stunned.

I've written more dreadful first drafts about the *Challenger* than probably anything else, too. Just about fifteen minutes ago I searched "challenger" on my hard drive and found two documents. One was a dreary, narrative poem that I wrote when I was an undergraduate and which I would never force on anybody. The other was this, a narrative that I almost don't remember writing. It's obvious to me that I wrote this as an example of some sort for my AP [advanced placement] students two school years ago, but I can't remember the details. Here it is, just as I found it.

The Kingdom Where Nobody Dies

"Childhood," the poem goes, "is the kingdom where nobody dies." I can't remember the first time I ever heard that, but let me tell you something—it's a lie. There is death in childhood, just as surely as there are rugburns, noogies, and Indian burns. That's what death is, really—the world's harshest Indian burn.

I learned about death on January 28, 1986, eight years old, a student in Ms. Selvaggi's third grade class. We lived in Orlando at the time, in a one-story bungalow in a brand-new subdivision outside of the city. We had a shimmering swimming pool in the back yard; in the front, a solitary orange tree grew from sandy soil. At the end of our street the houses and pavement gave way to a thicket of trees—the end of the suburbs, the end of civilization. My family moved there when we were young and struggling, at the edge of town on a plot of land that is now worth thousands more than it was then.

> Orlando had Disney World, EPCOT Center, and Sea World, but I didn't really care about those things. What Orlando really had was the space shuttle.

Orlando had Disney World, EPCOT Center, and Sea World, but I didn't really care about those things. What Orlando really had was the space shuttle.

Whenever the shuttle would launch from its pad in Cape Canaveral, my whole family would unfold the orange and brown lawn chairs with their latticework of frayed polyester and camp out on the front grass. Mom would make lemonade, and we'd keep our eyes trained on the horizon for the first glimpse of the shiny white marvel. I'd straddle my dirtbike at the end of the driveway, imagining the helmeted men at Mission Control (why they needed helmets at Mission Control seemed obvious to me, a vital detail whenever I pictured them) counting down. *Ten . . . nine . . . eight. . . .* I was right there with them, *seven . . . six . . . five. . . .* I could see the boosters begin to shudder. *Four . . . three . . . two . . . one . . . liftoff!*

And there it was! Silently peeking its head over the treetops! Rising, it seemed, on flames and an enormous pedestal of white smoke, the space shuttle! Mom would applaud, dad would hoot, and Adam, my little brother, would shove his fist into his mouth in celebration. We'd watch it climb into the sky, through the clouds, until it was just a tiny point at the end of a line, that enormous white pedestal elongated into a single beautiful stroke of white. Gone.

We had space shuttle magnets on our refrigerator. Here was *Discovery*, holding up a picture of my Aunt

Joyce, there was *Columbia* affixing a fifty-cent coupon for ground beef. I had space shuttles on my bedspread, photographs of *Atlantis* on my walls. At night, I put on my space shuttle pj's and did my spelling homework with space shuttle pencils. I didn't want to ride on the space shuttle; I wanted to *be* the space shuttle.

And there I was in Ms. Selvaggi's class, in January of 1986, everybody excited because today was the day that the teacher was going to go into space on the *Challenger*, and we were going to get to see it happen. Everybody in the country was paying attention to this flight, which made us proud and somewhat protective of our secret, that we got to watch these spaceships blast off over the rooftops of the suburbs and out of sight.

Ms. Selvaggi was young, in her early thirties, probably, and attractive. She was slender, had bright green eyes and long hair. She was Italian and looked it, and so naturally my mother and grandmother took a liking to her and often chatted with her after school, as the busses were chugging in the parking lot and we were waiting for my older brother to be dismissed.

She was a new teacher, and idealistic, and was always quick with a hug, a smile, or an extra gold star on my science homework. And I, a gifted child, knew how to supply all of the adorable smiles and precious answers that she could stand. She couldn't wait to talk to my mother at the end of the day—"You'll never guess what Aaron said today."

There was a solar eclipse that year, the year of the space shuttle. We made personal eclipse viewers out of cardboard shoe boxes and aluminum foil and marched out to the jungle gym behind the portables for a glimpse at the dangerous and irresistible solar eclipse. I trained my radiation-proof viewer to the eastern skies, to the same skies where the *Challenger* would later blow into pieces, and saw the moon crawl across the sun's flaming corona. I stood next to Ms. Selvaggi that day, and, though it might have been my imagination, it seemed that she wanted to witness this monumental event with me, her favorite student.

The Big Day

The day the *Challenger* exploded was freezing cold. Mom insisted we put on our coats and hats before she would drive us to school, it being much too bitter for the normal ten minute bike ride through the suburban streets and into the back lot of Dr. Phillips Elementary School. On the way, we kept our eyes open for orange trees dripping with icicles. Orange farmers would spray their crops with a garden hose whenever the temperature dropped below freezing so that the fruit would be protected by the insulating layer of ice. We had had sub-freezing temperatures that week, and had been treated to the bizarre sight of men wearing heavy winter jackets, spraying their icy orange trees with garden hoses.

> And how proud we were! We were from Florida. . . . Not everyone got to watch the space shuttle as it went up into space; in fact, many kids just our age didn't understand how special it was.

By the time I climbed the three wooden steps to the portable classroom and shed my coat and gloves, I had forgotten all about the cold. Ms. Selvaggi was keeping order in the small square room, but it was clear that everyone was excited. The T.V. in the corner was on, but the sound was down. [News anchor] Tom Brokaw's face filled the screen; he was intoning in what were surely grave words what a momentous day it was that an ordinary teacher from a high school in New Hampshire—Christa McAuliffe—was going into space.

And how proud we were! We were from Florida, Ms. Selvaggi reminded us. Not everyone got to watch the space shuttle as it went up into space; in fact, many kids just our age didn't understand how special it was that we got to watch it every time there was a launch. And this was such a special launch, when everyone in the country would be watching and wishing they were as lucky as we were because a teacher was going into space.

The morning was interminable. First was the Pledge of Allegiance, "America the Beautiful," and the morning announcements from Dr. Anderson, our blowhard of a vice-principal. Then the day started. Ms. Selvaggi got us right down to work on our reading, then vocabulary, and then our sentences. She managed to calm us down, though she kept looking at her watch.

Finally, it was after eleven o'clock. The intercom buzzed as it always did when we were about to have an important message from the principal.

"Good morning, boys and girls!" the voice rang through the speakers. "The first ever school teacher is about to go into space on the space shuttle! Everybody go out to the playground so we can see history being made!"

"Come on, everybody!" Ms. Selvaggi hollered. "Everyone in a single file line, now!"

No one thought of coats or gloves as we bounded out of our classroom, down the aisle of the other portables, and out toward the playground, where we had recently congregated for the thrilling glimpse of imminent death on the day when the moon passed between our own eyes and the sun.

When we made it to the playground, seconds later, most of us knew immediately what we were looking at. The shuttle had already exploded, and a bloated cloud hung in the sky where we should have seen a single line going straight out of sight. Even the dimmest of us needed only a few minutes to put it all together. First, we were too late to the launch to see the shuttle go into space. Second, something awful had happened. It was freezing

> Something awful had happened. It was freezing cold, we were standing on the playground in just our sweaters, and Christa McAuliffe was not going into space anymore.

cold, we were standing on the playground in just our sweaters, and Christa McAuliffe was not going into space anymore.

I looked at Ms. Selvaggi. When we were staring breathlessly at the solar eclipse earlier that schoolyear, she had seemed just like us, gazing in amazement at the show in the sky. Now, she was as shocked as I, staring at the horrible cloud in the clear, crisp morning.

Ms. Selvaggi didn't try to lie and tell us everything was going to be okay. She gathered her students together, some crying, some incredulous, and brought us back to the portable classroom. There was nothing she could do to change what had happened, and she didn't pretend to. She reached down and held me close as we walked back up the stairs to the portable. It was cold, and we both were shivering.

Watching Reports of the Disaster on British Television as a Young Boy

Simon Jones

In the following viewpoint, a British writer describes seeing news coverage of the *Challenger* disaster on television when he was a boy. No one who witnessed it will ever forget that day, he says. There were not many TV channels in the United Kingdom then, and only one news show was on when it happened—one that was meant for children. It was already covering the launch because of the teacher on board, so it broke the story before the other channels could prepare their news flashes. Soon, however, they interrupted their programming and played the tape of the apparent explosion over and over. Simon Jones is a British writer and blogger.

SOURCE. Simon Jones, "Challenger: 20 Years On," *Before I Forget*, January 28, 2006. Copyright © 2006 by Before I Forget. All rights reserved. Reproduced by permission.

It was a day that few who witnessed it on TV will ever forget; twenty years ago today [January 28, 2006] the space shuttle *Challenger*, the pride of the NASA fleet of three space shuttles, exploded seventy-four seconds after its launch, killing all seven crew including school teacher Christa McAuliffe, 37, who was picked from among 10,000 entries for a competition to be the first school teacher in space.

I can vividly recall the event. I was just a kid at the time, and I had just gotten in from school and fixed myself a drink before sitting in front of the TV. *Newsround*, a TV news show directed toward kids, was just starting. The presenter, Roger Finn, seemed unprepared—something unrehearsed was clearly happening, then pictures of the space shuttle were shown; something had clearly gone very wrong.

> Mom raced into the room and we both stood there transfixed by the pictures that were just being shown of the launch and then the horrific explosion.

At that point I stood up and ran to the living room door and shouted down the hallways to my Mom, who was in the kitchen. "Mom, the space shuttle has blown up!" Seconds later, still drying her hands on a dish cloth, Mom raced into the room and we both stood there transfixed by the pictures that were just being shown of the launch and then the horrific explosion.

TV Coverage of the Explosion

This was in the days before 24/7 news stations in the UK [United Kingdom], and at that point the only news on TV in the whole country across the 4 channels we had back then, was *Newsround*. Roger Finn knew it too, and his finely scripted news show for kids was set aside because history was unfolding right before everyone's eyes.

Pretty soon the other channels had interrupted their scheduled shows with news flashes. "Oh dear, this is terrible," my mom said as she sat down on the sofa with a very serious look on her face that reminded me of the look she had when the SAS [British special forces] swooped on the Iranian embassy in London, violently ending a siege in which terrorists had taken embassy staff hostage.

They showed the explosion over and over and over again, backward and forward, in normal speed and slow motion. The sound-byte that was forever to be etched into my memory that day was James D. Wetherbee of mission control in Houston saying "Challenger, go with throttle up" and shuttle Commander, Francis R. 'Dick' Scobee saying "Roger, go with throttle up." Moments later *Challenger* was engulfed in a fireball, the radio crackled and the two rockets tore off and flew aimlessly across a dark blue backdrop of the edge of space.

Roger Finn, at the time a new anchor for the *Newsround* show, later recalled the event.

> The *Challenger* explosion was not quite my first time in the *Newsround* chair—it was more like my sixth or so. Even so, you could see from the look on my face that I was plumbing new depths of stark fear. The news broke about fifteen minutes before we were on air, and an important principle was established: if a major news story broke during Children's programs then *Newsround* would break it. On this occasion I remember Julia Somerville (the main BBC news presenter) coming into the studio and some sort of "conversation" going on between Children's [programming] and News. Children's won and we did the newsflash.

This was the 25th launch of a space shuttle and was by now no longer a big event as far as news coverage was concerned. *Newsround* however was due to lead with the space shuttle's launch due to the fact that it was the first time a school teacher was going to space, and therefore it had a connection with the target audience of the show.

Seeing the Disaster in Person at Cape Canaveral as a Girl of Twelve

Yael Mermelstein

In the following viewpoint, an author recalls the day of the *Challenger* disaster. She was twelve years old and on the way to Disney World with her parents and sisters when they stopped at Kennedy Space Center to see the launch. Standing on the beach, they heard the voices of the astronauts on the broadcast system set up for the spectators. The crowd cheered when the shuttle lifted off. Then, watching it, she saw bursts of orange flame and plumes of smoke. The people around her were incredulous, and her parents could offer no answer to her questions. Soon her father took her away to Disney World, where people were walking around, smiling and laughing as if nothing had happened. The author could not put the tragedy out of her mind, and she still believes that people should not shut their eyes to the sad things in life. Yael Mermelstein is the author of several books and the winner of the Sydney Taylor Manuscript Award. She grew up in New York but now lives in Israel.

SOURCE. Yael Mermelstein, "Message in the Sky: When the Unthinkable Happens," *Aish.com*, February 2, 2008. Copyright © 2008 by Yael Mermelstein. All rights reserved. Reproduced by permission.

I don't remember much of the blurred watercolor of my childhood, but *that* day is indelibly marked in my memory.

"You know kids, there's a shuttle lift-off at Cape Canaveral today," my father said. We groaned. We were on a rather hyped up trip to Disneyworld, one that my family had waited years to take. Disney, Epcot, MGM—the world of fairy tale entertainment held no boundaries for us that week. For us three sisters, with me, then 12, the eldest, the space center wasn't much of a contender. But Daddy was always a fabulous educator, even on vacation.

"Okay kids!" my parents said excitedly. "Let's go to the Kennedy Space Center!" We drove down a long highway lined with yellow fields. It was January 28, 1986.

"Are you ready for take-off?" a voice asked into a microphone.

"We sure are," one of the astronauts answered on the broadcast system set up near the spectators.

I listened to the voices of the astronauts as I stood by the water's edge, peering into the infinite sky, imagining myself hurling through space on a rocket-ship. I had goose bumps.

"Rocket launchers ready?"

"Over."

I wondered which voice belonged to Christa McAuliffe. I had read all about her in my weekly reader at school. She was to be the first teacher in space. We had seen pictures of her training, floating in a weightless chamber. I craned my neck to see if I could find her family, but even my tiptoes didn't help. I could only see the spacecraft, mammoth and lonesome on a small island in the middle of the water.

A Burst of Orange

"10-9-8-7-6-5-4-3-2-1" The water was blue and the sky even bluer as the shuttle lifted off, leaving behind smoke like clouds of wadded cotton. The crowd cheered. My father smiled and clapped as he listened to the radio through his headphones. I saw a burst of orange on the right side of the craft.

"What was that?" I asked my father nervously.

"Just the rocket launcher separating," my father replied calmly.

Then there was another burst of orange, and two plumes of smoke arching through the air like flower petals. Then nothing.

"What happened?" I asked. My father fiddled nervously with his radio and everyone around began speaking in hushed tones, pointing, wondering.

"There seems to be a problem," my father said. He looked at my mother and squeezed my hand.

"This can't be." I heard one woman say. "No, impossible. There must be some sort of a mistake." But the unthinkable had happened. The *Challenger* had exploded, killing all seven astronauts on board.

> I imagined Christa McAuliffe floating in the weightless sky as my mouth clenched with fear.

I looked up, shielding my eyes, waiting to see some sign of life, but I could only see straggly lines of smoke falling like a newly hatched firecracker. I imagined Christa McAuliffe floating in the weightless sky as my mouth clenched with fear.

"Do you think the debris might fall on us?" I asked. I wondered where the astronauts were now.

The crowd dispersed amidst somber tones, some crying or leaning on each other for support.

"What happened?" my sisters asked.

"A very unfortunate thing happened sweetie," my father answered. We peppered our parents with questions, but what could they say? Eventually, we got back into our rental car.

Going to Disneyworld

"Come on kids," my father said with forced cheer. "Let's go to Disneyworld."

My sisters, ages six and seven, were able to move on rather quickly. I sat in the back seat, holding my stomach as it clenched and unclenched. *I just heard their voices*, I thought. *How could this have happened?*

I can still taste the feeling of walking around Disney World in a trance, watching the throngs picking off snatches of the pink cotton candy of life, while I had just returned from a bleak pit in history just miles away. *How*, I wondered, *could people move on so quickly? How could they smile and laugh in the face of such gruesomeness?*

> I can still [remember] walking around Disney World in a trance . . . while I had just returned from a bleak pit in history just miles away.

I rationalized to myself that these people did not have relatives aboard the craft. And they had not been there to see its disintegration. They were not haunted as I was by the cheerful sounds of the astronaut's voices moments before their collective demise. And so perhaps they were justified in their oblivion.

But there was something deeper at stake here.

When the children of Israel were taken out of Egypt and the Egyptians were drowning in the sea behind them, the Angels lifted up their voices and sang a song to God. The Medrash says that God rebuked them for their behavior. "My creatures are suffering and you sing songs?"

Catastrophes don't happen in a vacuum. We are all affected by them. If we bear witness to the suffering of God's creatures, some small part of us should take issue with blithely prancing through Disney a few miles away. Some small part of us should be wondering, "What does this mean to me?"

And as the 12-year-old me rode through Peter Pan's fantasy, I wondered, Why was I such an intimate witness to this tragedy? What am I meant to take out of this experience? Since I was there, I must be obligated to give more than just a moment of silence. It was a deeply disturbing thought, as I had no idea what to do.

Looking for Meaning

Life in this world is a multileveled experience, every physical experience reflecting a spiritually proportionate message. There are spiritual messages dangling all around us; all we have to do is reach our hands up and pluck them off the tree.

But we are sometimes too busy in Disneyworld to pay attention to the cues. As Rebbetzin Tzipporah Heller teaches, we are all often afflicted with the "Pass the Salt" syndrome. Imagine a dinner table:

"Can you believe it about the bomb in the school down the block?"

The Kennedy Space Center is located near the Atlantic Ocean in Cape Canaveral, Florida. The launch pads for the space shuttles can be seen in the distance. Spectators could watch shuttle launches from official viewing platforms at the center and from many beaches near the area. (© **Corbis**.)

"Yeah. I heard the explosion all the way here. Crazy that there was nobody in the school at that moment. Five minutes later and it would have been a disaster."

"Whew. Yeah. Could you please pass the salt?"

'Pass the Salt' is how we pass the buck on spiritual change.

But what if we decided to take it one step further?

I witnessed something inspiring, difficult, cataclysmic —and there is a message in this for me. Maybe I should be more grateful for my own life? Maybe I need to appreciate the people in my life more? Maybe there is a change in me that is begging to be made?

The way that we react to the awesome things that happen in the world around us, speaks volumes about who we really are.

> "Witnessing the *Challenger* disaster was a first step for me in grasping the ephemeral nature of life.

Witnessing the *Challenger* disaster was a first step for me in grasping the ephemeral nature of life. It was a difficult and distressing topic to assimilate, but it was the beginning of a quest which led me to more intense religious commitment. I couldn't shut it out of my mind and I'm glad that I didn't.

When the world around us seems chaotic, let's open up our eyes really wide. We may just see the writing on the wall that was meant just for us. After all, life can provide a whole lot of flavor even without the salt.

A Teacher Describes Watching the Disaster on Television at School

Victor Lana

In the following viewpoint, a former teacher describes how he felt on the day of the *Challenger* accident. The shuttle flight was important to him, because he had applied to be the teacher in space. His mom had thought it was crazy, yet he had wanted to do it because he had always been excited by television shows and films about space travel. At first, after not being selected, he had envied Christa McAuliffe; yet, it had become a source of pride for all teachers that she was so famous. On the day of the flight, he thought about her going into space while he was teaching an English lesson. There was no TV in his classroom, but a class down the hall was watching, and suddenly he heard crying coming from there. Then the principal announced the disaster over the intercom. Fighting his own tears, he said something to his students about her bravery, although he knew it could not bring them any comfort. Now, twenty-five years later, he believes she will remain an inspiration forever. Victor Lana is a school principal as well as the author of several books and articles.

SOURCE. Victor Lana, "The Challenger Explosion: A Teacher Recalls That Fateful Day," *BlogCritics.org*, January 28, 2011. Copyright © 2011 by BlogCritics.org. All rights reserved. Reproduced by permission.

January 1986. It's kind of like November 1963 or December 1941 or September 2001. The *Challenger* explosion was a news event that not only overwhelmed people with its impact but created a lasting impression and inspired the inevitable "Where were you?" question. Those of us who remember that day 25 years ago will never forget the time and place we heard about this terrible moment in the collective memory of our nation.

I was a seventh grade teacher in a Catholic school in Queens, NY. Although I taught English classes, I spoke about the *Challenger* blastoff with my students in the weeks before the launch. Besides the obvious applications to science and math connected to such an event, I found there was an extremely tangible literary element to space travel. Had not space voyages been the subject of stories and poems? Each time I watched a craft takeoff, I felt awash in the lyrical countdown that was poetic as it was methodical.

There was also another connection I had to the *Challenger*: I had submitted an application to the Teacher in Space Program that would eventually land Christa McAuliffe in the *Challenger* on January 28, 1986. I recall it was a long application, filled out a couple of years before when I was a rookie teacher. Although I figured I didn't stand a chance against all the scientific types that probably would be chosen, I still sent it in because I believed in taking every opportunity. Besides, if I were selected, it would fulfill all my boyhood Captain Kirk dreams to—if not boldly go where no man had gone before—be floating around in the velvet black of space and looking down at the hazy blue marble Earth.

Of course, I was not selected and I never told my students about it. I had told my family and I remember my Mom thinking I was crazy. "Who would want to do a thing like that?" she asked. Well, I wanted to do it because it would be the stuff of all the tales I had ever read and all the TV shows and films I had seen about space travel. I would write about it and maybe even star in a television show later on—something like *Teacher in Space*.

We all know that many educators applied for this opportunity of a lifetime, but in the end Christa McAuliffe was chosen as the teacher who would go on the voyage. Though I envied her at first, I grew to accept not going and also to embrace the fact that one of my own would be making this fantastic voyage. It was a source of great pride for all us earthbound teachers, for we saw the adulation and respect that people everywhere had, not just for Christa, but for teachers in general now that she had become so famous.

> "Christa McAuliffe was chosen as the teacher who would go on the voyage. . . . It was a source of great pride for all us earthbound teachers.

A Day of Sorrow

So on that fateful day I was teaching a lesson about transitive and intransitive verbs. I probably sighed a little bit, glanced at my watch, and thought about Christa taking off for the heavens while I was stuck with my feet firmly planted on the ground teaching something most of my students found boring. In those days we didn't have televisions in every classroom, but I knew one of the science teachers had signed out the only one we had on a rolling cart on our floor. She and her class were watching the liftoff down the hall. My students worked on a few examples in their notebooks and the serene quiet was suddenly broken by a kind of crying and moaning that floated through the doorway, a sort of crush of recognition that something horrible happened.

In a few moments the principal's stoic voice came over the classroom intercom announcing, "The *Challenger* Space Shuttle has exploded on takeoff. Please pray for those on board and their families and friends." Once she stopped speaking, I heard my students gasping, some staring out the window as if they thought they'd see falling pieces of the ship coming down from the sky.

What do you say in moments like this? Sometimes silence is the best thing, and I just sat on the edge of my desk and stared at them as they buzzed their conversations and cried tears. I waited for a time and then one of the girls (who had been following Christa's journey diligently and had written about it in her journal) looked up at me and asked the question I had no answer for: "Mr. Lana, why did this happen?"

> Not even the explosion that took her life could destroy the power of the example [Christa McAuliffe] set for teachers and students in America and all over the world.

Twenty-five years have passed and I still don't have the answer. At the time I think I stammered a bit, fighting my own tears, and said something about God's plan and Christa's bravery. I honestly don't remember what I said anymore, and I'm not sure if it brought any comfort to my students. I do know that nothing brought any comfort to me: not that day or a long time afterwards.

I remember staring at the cold winter sky that night so long ago, staring up at the constellation Orion so bold and bright in the dark night sky. I thought how I had submitted that application and wanted to really go, but so did so many others. Christa went for all of us, all the teachers who worked so hard every day, who loved their jobs and their students as much as anything in life. That kind of dedication and spirit sent Christa McAuliffe up in that Space Shuttle, and not even the explosion that took her life could destroy the power of the example she set for teachers and students in America and all over the world.

So tonight I looked up at the sky again, but I couldn't see Orion or anything else because there was a cloudy sky, ready to drop more snow on us. Still, I could see the trail that she blazed that day, and though she's gone, her memory remains and her name will forever linger in the firmament, inspiring us now and forevermore with her bold desire to reach for the stars.

GLOSSARY

Columbia One of the five space shuttles. It was lost in an accident that occurred on February 1, 2003.

ET External tank—on the space shuttle, the large liquid fuel tank that supplies oxygen and hydrogen to main engines during launch.

KSC Kennedy Space Center at Cape Canaveral, Florida—the shuttle launch site.

LCC Launch Control Center.

MSFC Marshall Space Flight Center, a NASA installation in Huntsville, Alabama. It was responsible for the manufacture, assembly, and operation of the space shuttle's propulsion elements—the main engine, external tank, and solid rocket boosters.

NASA National Aeronautics and Space Administration.

O-ring A flexible doughnut-shaped ring of rubber or synthetic material used as a gasket to seal a joint. On the space shuttle, O-rings were used between sections of the solid rocket boosters.

Orbiter or OV The STS vehicle that orbited and landed, commonly called the space shuttle, although officially "space shuttle" referred to the entire STS at launch, including the portions that were jettisoned.

Rogers Commission The presidential commission appointed to investigate the *Challenger* accident.

RTLS Return to Launch Site, a planned emergency procedure for a shuttle following a failure that does not kill the crew.

SRBs Solid Rocket Boosters—on the space shuttle, the twin rockets flanking the large external fuel tank that burn solid fuel during first minutes of ascent and then drop off, parachuting into the ocean.

STS   Space Transportation System, consisting of the orbiter vehicle (OV), its external fuel tank (ET), and its twin solid rocket boosters (SRBs).

STS-51-L   The official mission designation for the *Challenger* flight that failed.

Thiokol   Morton Thiokol, the company that produced the solid rocket boosters for the space shuttles.

TIS   Teacher in Space program.

CHRONOLOGY

1985 July 19: Christa McAuliffe's selection from among eleven thousand applicants to be the first teacher in space is announced. In September, she begins training.

1986 January 24: The scheduled *Challenger* launch is postponed because of bad weather at the abort landing site.

January 25: The launch is postponed again because of predicted bad weather at Kennedy Space Center.

January 27: The launch is scrubbed for a third time because of a stuck bolt on *Challenger*'s hatch, plus increasing cross winds.

January 27–28: During the night, NASA managers decide to launch in the morning despite freezing weather, over the objections of two rocket engineers.

January 28: At 11:38 A.M. EST *Challenger* is launched. Seventy-three seconds into the flight, it breaks apart. After another 2 minutes 45 seconds, the crew cabin hits the ocean, killing the astronauts, some of whom may have been unconscious prior to impact.

January 28: At 5 P.M. EST President Ronald Reagan addresses the nation on television.

January 31: A memorial service for the *Challenger* crew is held at Johnson Space Center in Houston, at which President Reagan again speaks.

February 3: The appointment of a presidential commission to investigate the *Challenger*, known as the Rogers Commission, is announced.

March 8: The crew cabin and remains of the crew are found and recovered from the ocean.

April 29: The identified remains of the astronauts are returned to their families for burial.

May 20: The unidentified remains are buried in Arlington National Cemetery beneath a memorial to all seven astronauts.

June 9: The report of the Rogers Commission's investigation is released.

June and July: The Committee on Science and Technology of the US House of Representatives holds hearings to investigate the *Challenger* accident.

July 28: NASA releases the transcript of a recovered and restored tape of communications between flight controllers and *Challenger* during its last seconds before breakup. A report on the death of the astronauts by biomedical specialist Joseph Kerwin is also released, publicly admitting for the first time that they were not killed instantly when *Challenger* broke apart.

1988 September 29: After more than two years of redesign and retesting, space shuttle flights resume with the launch of *Discovery*.

1990 December 8: After a long court battle over a lawsuit filed by the *New York Times*, a federal appeals court rules that NASA need not release the audio tape of the last communication of the astronauts aboard *Challenger*.

2003   February 1: The space shuttle *Columbia* is destroyed during reentry due to damage to its left wing caused by a piece of external tank insulation that had fallen off during launch. All seven astronauts aboard are killed.

2004   July 23: The lost *Challenger* and *Columbia* astronauts are posthumously awarded the Congressional Space Medal of Honor by President George W. Bush.

FOR FURTHER READING

Books

Randy Avera, *The Truth About Challenger*. Good Hope, GA: Randolph, 2003.

Colin Burgess, *Teacher in Space: Christa McAuliffe and the Challenger Legacy*. Lincoln, NE: University of Nebraska Press, 2000.

Richard C. Cook, *Challenger Revealed: An Insider's Account of How the Reagan Administration Caused the Greatest Tragedy of the Space Age*. New York: Basic Books, 2007.

Grace George Corrigan, *A Journal for Christa: Christa McAuliffe, Teacher in Space*. Lincoln, NE: University of Nebraska Press, 2000.

Ben Evans, *Space Shuttle Challenger: Ten Journeys into the Unknown*. New York: Springer, 2006.

Richard P. Feynman, *What Do You Care What Other People Think? Further Adventures of a Curious Character*. New York: Norton, 1988.

Sue L. Hamilton, *Space Shuttle Challenger*. Bloomington, MN: Abdo, 1988.

Robert T. Hohler, *I Touch the Future: The Story of Christa McAuliffe*. New York: Random House, 1986.

Richard S. Lewis, *The Last Voyage of Challenger*. New York: Columbia University Press, 1988.

Malcolm McConnell, *Challenger: A Major Malfunction*. New York: HarperCollins, 1988.

Allan J. McDonald and James R. Hansen, *Truth, Lies, and O-Rings: Inside the Space Shuttle Challenger Disaster*. Gainesville, FL: University Press of Florida, 2009.

Report of the Presidential Commission on the Space Shuttle Challenger Accident. Washington, DC: US Government Printing Office, 1986.

Mary E. Stuckey, *Slipping the Surly Bonds: Reagan's Challenger Address.* College Station, TX: Texas A&M University Press, 2006.

Joseph J. Trento, *Prescription for Disaster: From the Glory of Apollo to the Betrayal of the Shuttle.* New York: Crown, 1987.

Diane Vaughan, *The Challenger Launch Decision: Risky Technology, Culture, and Deviance at NASA.* Chicago: University of Chicago Press, 1997.

Washington Post Staff, *Challengers: The Inspiring Life Stories of the Seven Brave Astronauts of Shuttle Mission 51-L.* New York: Pocket Books, 1986.

Periodicals and Internet Sources

David Baker, "Science Crashed with Challenger," *New Scientist,* January 29, 1987.

Melinda Beck, "NASA's Troubled Flight Plan: There's No Turning Back, But Are We on the Right Path?," *Newsweek,* February 10, 1986.

Wayne Biddle, "NASA: What's Needed to Put It on Its Feet?," *Discover,* January 1987.

William F. Buckley Jr., "Ease Up on the Challenger," *National Review,* March 28, 1986.

Marcia Dunn, "Space Shuttle Challenger Explosion: 25 Years Later, a Still Painful Wound," *Huffington Post,* January 28, 2011. www.huffingtonpost.com.

Jonathan Eberhart, "Challenger Disaster Muddles NASA's Future," *Science News,* March 15, 1986.

Richard P. Feynman, "An Outsider's Inside View of the Challenger Inquiry," *Physics Today,* February 1988.

"5 Myths of Challenger Disaster Debunked," *National Geographic,* January 27, 2011. http://news.nationalgeographic.com.

Malcolm Gladwell, "Blowup," *New Yorker,* January 22, 1996.

Peter Grier, "Challenger Explosion: How President Reagan Reacted," *Christian Science Monitor,* January 28, 2011. www.csmonitor.com.

Timothy E. Kline, "Walking on Wings: Caution and Courage for Manned Space Flight," *Air University Review*, May–June 1986.

Henry Lansford, "Phoenix in Space: Rising from the Ashes to Orbit," *World & I*, December 1990.

Ruth A. Lewis and John S. Lewis, "Getting Back on Track in Space," *Technology Review*, August–September 1986.

Life, "The Challenger Disaster–10 Years Later," January 26, 1996.

Life, "Whistle-Blowers," March 1988.

Ed Magnuson, "Putting Schedule over Safety: Despite Challenger, the Shuttle Program Ignores Whistle-Blowers," *Time*, February 1, 1988.

Eliot Marshall, "Feynman Issues His Own Shuttle Report, Attacking NASA's Risk Estimates," *Science*, June 27, 1986.

Jon D. Miller, "The Challenger Accident and Public Opinion: Attitudes Toward the Space Programme in the USA," *Space Policy*, May 1987.

Ivars Peterson, "The Last, Tragic Mission of Challenger," *Science News*, February 1, 1986.

Dennis E. Powell, "Obviously, A Major Malfunction," *Miami Herald*, November 13, 1988.

Daniel Riffe and James Glen Stovall, "Diffusion of News of Shuttle Disaster: What Role for Emotional Response," *Journalism Quarterly*, Autumn 1989.

Hugh Sidey, "Pioneers in Love with the Frontier," *Time*, February 10, 1986.

Timothy Stenovek, "New Challenger Video: Rare Footage of 1986 Disaster Uncovered," *Huffington Post*, May 1, 2012. www.huffingtonpost.com.

Rajini Vaidyanathan, "Challenger: The Shuttle Disaster That Shook the World," *BBC News Magazine*, January 28, 2011. www.bbc.co.uk.

Louden Wainright, "After 25 Years: An End to Innocence," *Life*, March 1986.

John C. Wright et al., "How Children Reacted to Televised Coverage of the Space Shuttle Disaster," *Journal of Communication*, Spring 1989.

Websites

Challenger Center for Space Education (www.challenger.org). This is the official website of the organization founded by the families of the *Challenger* astronauts to inspire kids to learn about science and technology.

Challenger Disaster (www.history.com/topics/challenger -disaster). This website offers a brief summary of the disaster and its aftermath, plus several videos.

Challenger Disaster Remembered (http://www.boston.com /bigpicture/2011/01/challenger_disaster_25_years_l.html). This site highlights a series of photos compiled on the twenty-fifth anniversary of the *Challenger* disaster to honor the memory of the crew.

Challenger STS 51-L Accident (http://history.nasa.gov/sts511 .html). This site provides detailed information about *Challenger*, including reports, movie clips, and the transcript of the last communications from the crew.

Report of the Presidential Commission on the Space Shuttle Challenger Accident (http://history.nasa.gov/rogers rep/511cover.htm). The full official report of the Rogers Commission.

Roger Boisjoly–The Challenger Disaster (www.onlineethics .org/cms/7123.aspx). The Online Ethics Center for Engineering and Research offers material from the rocket engineer who foresaw the failure of the O-rings and tried to prevent the launch.

INDEX

161

N